ANUNNAKI BIBLE
THE CUNEIFORM SCRIPTURES
NEW STANDARD ZUIST EDITION

POCKET EDITION

Published from
Mardukite Borsippa HQ, Monte Vista, Colorado
Founding Church of Mardukite Zuism
& Systemology Society

Graphics Assistance by Kyra Kaos

ANUNNAKI BIBLE

THE CUNEIFORM SCRIPTURES

NEW STANDARD ZUIST EDITION

Developed by Joshua Free for the
Church of Mardukite Zuism

© 2021, JOSHUA FREE

ISBN : 978-0-578-85669-8

No part of this publication may be reproduced in any form or by any means, electronic or mechanical, including photocopying, recording, or any information storage or retrieval system, without permission from the publisher. This book is not intended to substitute medical treatment or advice.

*An abridged pocket version of
The Complete Anunnaki Bible
edited for founding the
Church of Mardukite Zuism*

Pocket Paperback Edition — March 2021

Also available in hardcover

mardukite.com

The _Original_ Anunnaki Cuneiform Bible

Here is the ancient Sumerian Anunnaki origins of all known religious systems on Earth today.

Here is the cuneiform tablet origin of the Judeo-Christian, Hermetic and Zoroastrian texts; records that predate better-known scriptures of the "Holy Bible" by 2,000 years!

Here is the "original" Anunnaki Bible —separating "prehistory" from "history"— collecting the oldest writings on the planet from Babylonian sources in Mesopotamia.

Here is the recovery and incorporation of wisdom from the Ancient Near East into a modern tradition of Babylonian Neopaganism known for over a decade as Mardukite Zuism.

The Mardukite Anunnaki Bible Zuist Edition represents concise historic archaeological foundations for a new generation of Chamberlains, Mardukite Ministers, Zuist Priests and Priestesses, and other Systemologists around the world.

Here is the New Standard Zuist Edition of the classic text by world renowned Joshua Free; an abridged version of "The Complete Anunnaki Bible" edited for the Church of Mardukite Zuism.

TABLET OF CONTENTS

Publisher's Preface to this Edition . . . 10

MARDUKITE ZUISM:
A BRIEF INTRODUCTION
- Cuneiform Tablets . . . 15
- Systems: Life, Universes & Everything . . . 17
- Basic Definitions (*Mardukite Zuism*) . . . 18
- The Babylonian Creation Epic . . . 21
- Tablets of Destiny and Self-Honesty . . . 23
- Ladder of Lights: Gateways to Infinity . . . 25
- Cosmology and Metaphysics . . . 25
- Systemology and Spirituality . . . 27
- The Highest Form of Divine Worship . . . 29
- Utilitarian Ethics (*Mardukite Zuism*) . . . 30
- "Zu" and Modern Zuist Religion . . . 31
- Goals and Ideals (*Mardukite Zuism*) . . . 32
- Infinity, God and Supreme Beingness . . . 33
- The True Human Alpha-Spirit . . . 34
- Practices of Spiritual Counseling . . . 36
- Principles of Belief (*Mardukite Zuism*) . . . 38
- Marduk's Tablet of Destiny . . . 41

THE OLD TESTAMENT
OF ANUNNAKI GODS OF THIS UNIVERSE
- Epic of Creation (*Enuma Eliš*) . . . 45
- The Fifty Names of Marduk . . . 62
- Apocrypha of the Marduk Tablet . . . 70

- Kingship of the Ancient Ones ... 72
- The Rise of the Gods of Earth ... 73
- Creation of Human Forms (*Adamu*) ... 76
- Wise One Among Humans (*Adapa*) ... 80
- Of the Generations of Adapa on Earth ... 87
- Secrets of Seth (Sati), Son of Adapa ... 88
- Marduk Loses Kingship in Heaven ... 91
- Kingship on Earth (*King-Lists extract*) ... 93
- Ishtar's Descent to the Underworld ... 93
- Prelude to Atra-Asis (*King Lists*) ... 110
- The Disposal of Humanity (*Atra-Asis*) ... 110

THE NEW TESTAMENT
OF PRIESTS AND KINGS ON THIS EARTH

- Atra-Asis Addendum (*King-Lists*) ... 117
- The World Order of Enki ... 118
- Prelude to the Akkadians (*King-Lists*) ... 123
- Enlilship of Marduk on Earth ... 127
- The Sargon Tablet ... 129
- Lament for Babylon & The Last Days of Earth ... 130
- Mardukite Kingship in Babylon ... 133
- Law of Marduk Tablet (*Hammurabi*) ... 133
- Nergal Attacks Babylon (*Erra Epos*) ... 139
- Epilogos of Ishum (*Erra Epos*) ... 146
- The First Tablet of Nabu-Tutu ... 147
- The Second Tablet of Nabu-Tutu ... 150
- The Third Tablet of Nabu-Tutu ... 153
- Prelude to Chaldeo-Assyrians ... 156

- The Nebuchadnezzar II Tablet . . . 158
- A Dragon-King's Prayer to Marduk . . . 159
- Capture of Babylon With the Favor of Marduk . . . 160
- The Priest-King's Tablet of Wisdom . . . 163

APPENDIX
- The Chaldean Oracles . . . 167
- The Sajaha Oracles . . . 185

Additional Studies . . . 216

PUBLISHER'S PREFACE TO THE NEW STANDARD ZUIST EDITION

Now, more than a decade since the "Mardukite Core" materials by Joshua Free began circulating in the underground, a new edition of the cornerstone volume has arrived, uncovering ancient cuneiform scriptures from the heart of Mesopotamia and revealing the near-prehistoric legacy of the Sumerians and Babylonians as never before.

The purpose of the "NSZE" version of the *Anunnaki Bible* is to simplify a new futurist presentation of the original cuneiform tablet translations from *The Complete Anunnaki Bible* —the result of over half-of-a-decade of intensive explorations by the Mardukite Research Organization (Mardukite Chamberlains/Council of Nabu) from 2008-2015.

For the first time in the modern history, humanity can access this collection of the most concise *cuneiform scripture* translations available—composing, themselves, the most ancient "Bible" known to mankind; and one that went on to inspire the religious and spiritual systems on the planet Earth for thousands of years thereafter.

This edition of the *Anunnaki Bible* presents a "new standard" for officially incorporating a solid modern religious tradition of "Mardukite Zuism" philosophy and its Systemology of applied spiritual technology for the future.

Great care was taken in selecting and arranging the most critical elements of ancient Mesopotamian literature to present this universally workable edition (once exclusively a "Mardukite" version of these materials). In doing so, this special *Anunnaki Bible NSZE* applies equally to all modern factions, revival/reconstruction efforts, historical or academic pursuits and Mesopotamian Neopaganism. To aid study and research, a Seeker may still refer to *The Complete Anunnaki Bible* for supplemental commentary.

In addition to *The Complete Anunnaki Bible*, the Founding Church of Mardukite Zuism & Systemology Society distributes materials (books, audio lecture CDs, &tc,) by Joshua Free as produced by the Mardukite Academy of Systemology to assist a Seeker in progressing on the *Pathway*. If you were gifted this book by an individual, consider asking them more about it.

MARDUKITE ZUISM

A BRIEF INTRODUCTION

*According to the most ancient
historical records
written at the birth of our
modern civilization...*

432,000 YEARS AGO...[*]

a small population of advanced beings—called the <u>ANUNNAKI</u>—began developing the planet Earth for their purposes. These elite Self-Actualized spiritual beings resided on Earth in physical bodies, but found their forms inadequate for the physical labors required. Enter: the "Human Condition." Ancient "<u>cuneiform</u>" tablet writings from Sumerians and Babylonians of Mesopotamia are clear regarding the original creation and systematic programming of Humanity.

CUNEIFORM...

is the oldest known writing system used by scribes of ancient Babylon to record their wisdom and the history of humanity on <u>clay tablets</u>. "Cuneiform" is named for its style of wedge-shaped script formed by a <u>reed pen</u> called a "<u>stylus.</u>" Rather than an alphabet of letters, cuneiform is a system of "<u>signs</u>" representing "things" and "ideas." These may be combined to represent even more complex "signs."

---

[*] First published in 2019 as "*Mardukite Zuism: A Brief Introduction.*"

Many concepts adopted for modern "<u>Mardukite Zuism</u>" are derived from cuneiform tablets. The ANUNNAKI introduced complex writing systems in order to program civilization and all parameters of Reality for the Human Condition. Legendary "<u>Tablets of Destiny</u>" (Divine Truth, supreme knowledge and cosmic power of the "gods") were first introduced to Humanity in the Babylonian narrative known best as the "<u>Epic of Creation</u>.

THE ARCANE TABLETS.

Ancient Babylonians used the Tablets of Destiny & Creation Epic to systematize all cosmic knowledge into a workable <u>paradigm</u> called "Mardukite Zuism"—a <u>systemology</u> received directly from the ANUNNAKI.

> <u>Paradigm</u> : an all-encompassing standard or religion used to view the world and communicate reality.
>
> <u>Systemology</u> : applied philosophies of Mardukite Zuism combined with personal spiritual techniques and technology ("Tech") that is effectively demonstrating systematic principles of a "paradigm."

THE EPIC OF CREATION.

Seven cuneiform tablets compose the ancient <u>Babylonian Epic of Creation</u>, named the <u>Enuma Eliš</u> by scholars after its opening lines. These seven tablets are the basis for what later traditions refer to as the *"Seven Days of Creation."* The *Epic of Creation* tablets describe development of all existences with a Divine artistic perfection. The Enuma Eliš is the core example of religious literature from Babylon, which served as the basis for ancient *"Mardukite Zuism"*—the first true systematized religion in history.

THE SYSTEMOLOGY OF LIFE, UNIVERSES & EVERYTHING.

The *Arcane Tablets* describe the division of the ALL by the LAW, outside of which is but IN-FINITY. The *Epic of Creation* describes these activities as "mythology."

The Mardukite Systemology "Standard Model" uses the same information to demonstrates...

that <u>ALL</u> ("AN-KI") envelops both:
the <u>Spiritual Existences</u> ("AN")
and the <u>Physical Existences</u> ("KI")
divided by <u>Cosmic Law</u> and
connected by <u>Life-Awareness</u> ("ZU")
and beyond which is only the <u>Abyss</u>,
an <u>Infinity of Nothingness</u> ("ABZU").

ANCIENT SUMERIAN DEFINITIONS.

<u>ABZU</u> = "Abyss" ("Nothingness")
<u>ZU</u> = "Spiritual Life" ("Awareness")
<u>ANKI</u> = "All Existences" ("Existence")
<u>AN</u> = "Spiritual Universe" ("Heaven")
<u>KI</u> = "Physical Universe" ("Earth")

ALTERNATE MARDUKITE NEXGEN SYSTEMOLOGY DEFINITIONS.

<u>ABZU</u> = "Infinity of Nothingness"
<u>ZU</u> = "Awareness of Alpha Spirit"
<u>ANKI</u> = "The Standard Model"
<u>AN</u> = "Alpha Existence" ("Spiritual")
<u>KI</u> = "Beta Existence" ("Physical")

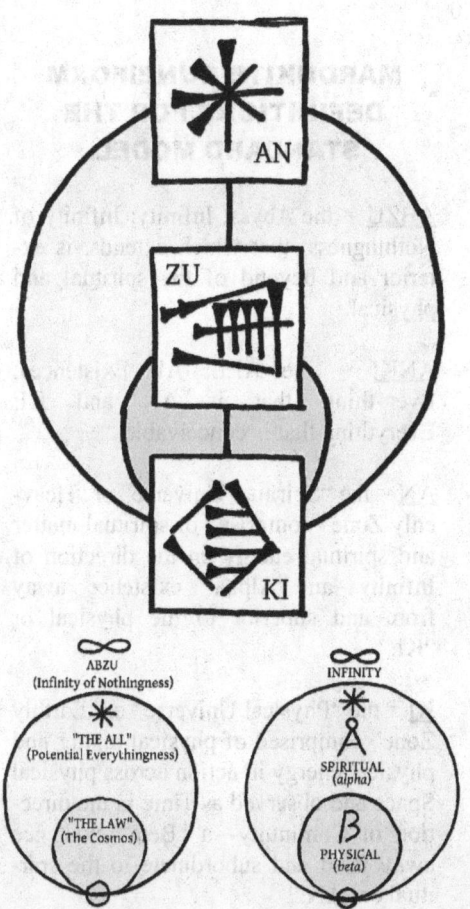

MARDUKITE CUNEIFORM DEFINITIONS FOR THE STANDARD MODEL.

<u>ABZU</u> = the Abyss; Infinity; Infinity of Nothingness; that which extends, is exterior and beyond of the spiritual and physical.

<u>ANKI</u> = the ALL; All Existences; Everything that is AN and KI; Everything that is conceivable.

<u>AN</u> = the "Spiritual Universe" or "Heavenly Zone" comprised of spiritual matter and spiritual energy, in the direction of Infinity—an "Alpha" existence away from and superior to the physical or "KI."

<u>KI</u> = the "Physical Universe" or "Earthly Zone" comprised of physical matter and physical energy in action across physical Space and observed as Time in the direction of Continuity—a "Beta" existence away from and subordinate to the spiritual or "AN."

<u>ZU</u> = "to know"; "knowingness"; "Awareness" or "consciousness"; spiritual energy and matter of AN that is observed as "Lifeforce" in KI; "Spiritual Life Energy"; the actual personal spiritual Identity or "Awareness" of Self as Spirit which extends along a "line" from the Spiritual Universe (AN) to the Physical Universe (KI).

THE TABLETS OF DESTINY & BABYLONIAN CREATION EPIC.

The Absolute behind ALL Existence is referred to on the *Tablets of Destiny* as the Infinity of Nothingness. It is the only constant static of latent unmanifest potentiality of ALL and Everythingness.

The LAW—Cosmic Law—is defined as the Cosmic Dragon—TIAMAT—on "Epic of Creation" Tablets. She is the First Cause or movement across a "Sea of Infinity." Later, the LAW becomes a division between Spiritual Existence ("AN") and any Physical Universe ("KI"). The LAW—Tiamat—permeating ALL, uses the *Tablets of Destiny* and then fixes the systems of finite potential: The Systems of Manifestation—Substance, Motion and Awareness.

"Before heaven or earth are named," the formation and interaction of active existences —"substances" and "bodies" and "Life" and "gods"—creates turbulence and waves of action through space. The governing system of Cosmic Law—Tiamat—responds accordingly. She fixes the Tablets of Destiny to her "deputy"—a messenger wave action of the LAW named "Kingu" and sends him rippling out to "meet" the Anunnaki "gods."

The Anunnaki Assembly of "gods" prepare to battle The LAW. When none among them comes forth to engage, it is the Anunnaki "god" MARDUK that volunteers as hero to confront Kingu and Tiamat—but with a condition that the Anunnaki Assembly recognize him as "Chief of the Gods" upon his success.

When MARDUK approaches the LAW directly, he is flanked by Kingu and the "army of Ancient Ones." MARDUK is able to relinquish the Tablets of Destiny from Kingu. With the Tablets of Destiny, Marduk conquers a true understanding of Cosmic Law and thereby Tiamat.

THE TABLETS OF DESTINY & SELF-HONESTY.

Marduk uses the Tablets of Destiny to discover "Self-Honesty" and Divine Knowledge governing "Cosmic Ordering"—systems dividing the "Spiritual Universe" (AN) from a "Physical Universe" (KI). The two universes are connected only by a stream of Spiritual Lifeforce Awareness that Sumerians called ZU. Wisdom from the Arcane Tablets is later passed down to and concealed by an ancient esoteric secret society in Babylon: the Scribes, High Priests and Priestesses of Mardukite Zuism.

Self-Honesty is a term describing an original "Alpha" state of clear knowingness and Self-directed beingness. "Self-Honesty" is the most basic and true expression of Self as "I-AM"—free of artificial attachments; reactive-response conditioning; and imposed or enforced programming as Reality for the Human Condition. Spiritual development in modern *Mardukite Zuism* is referred to as the "Pathway to Self-Honesty" and the "Gateway to Infinity." It is modeled directly from the Ancient Mystery Tradition observed at the Temples of Babylon.

THE KEY TO THE GATE.

"I will take my Blood—and with Bone—I will fashion a Race of Humans to keep Watch of the Gate. And from the Blood of Kingu I will create another Race of Humans to inhabit the Earth in service to the Gods—so shrines to the Anunnaki may be built and the temples filled. I will bind the Elder Gods to the Watchtowers; let them keep watch over the Gate of Abzu and the Gate of Tiamat and Gate of Kingu—and with a Key that shall be ever hidden, known to none, except only to my Mardukites." —MARDUK, *Enuma Elis, Creation Tablet VI.*

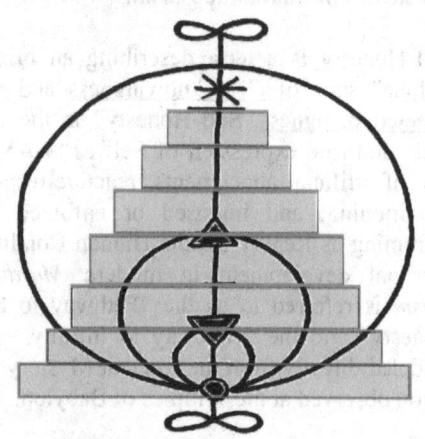

THE ANUNNAKI LADDER OF LIGHTS & BABYLONIAN GATEWAYS TO INFINITY.

<u>ZIGGURAT TEMPLES</u> in Babylonia—and throughout Mesopotamia—served to remind populations of the ZU connecting "Heaven" and "Earth."

Seven-stepped "levels" of the physical <u>ZIGGURAT TEMPLES</u> of Babylonia—and seven corresponding Gates—represent spiritual levels of actualized Awareness; states of Self-purification (or "spiritual defragmentation") as they ascend in the direction of AN toward Infinity of Supreme Beingness—the Pathway of Self-Honesty—in imitation of the footsteps of the gods during their descent through the "spheres" or "Gates."

COSMOLOGY AND METAPHYSICS.

All Things in the Physical Universe are in motion—wave motions of "energy and matter in space measured as-and-across time." Continuity of the Physical Universe (KI) is divided by LAW and encompassed by the ALL (ANKI).

The direction of AN extends toward ABZU, an Infinity of Nothingness beyond effective existence.

The true <u>Alpha Self</u> is a source—the "spiritual cause" of "physical effects." It engages a <u>Self-determined WILL</u> from its "spiritual" <u>Alpha existence</u> to actualize Awareness for "physical" <u>Beta existence</u> experience as "Life."

USING ANCIENT WISDOM TO UNLOCK HUMAN POTENTIAL.

Communication of clear wisdom and true knowledge from Arcane Tablets is distorted as it passes through time and geography, diverse languages and authoritarian cultures using the "Power" to program the masses and fragment the Human Condition away from Self-Honesty.

Use of this ancient wisdom reveals the Keys to "<u>Cosmic Ordering</u>"—applying the highest Self-directed understanding of "cause-and-effect" sequences in the Physical Universe.

MARDUKITE ZUISM, SYSTEMOLOGY & SPIRITUALITY.

The Spiritual Universe (AN)—of metaphysical or spiritual energy and metaphysical or spiritual matter is not dependent on the Physical Universe (KI) to exist; the two are existentially independent of each other, maintaining a single channel, conduit or connection, which is <u>Alpha Spirit</u> "Awareness" as Spiritual Life or ZU. The Alpha Spirit engages a <u>ZU-line</u>, a spiritual lifeline of ZU energy to a genetic vehicle or organic body to experience physical beta existence.

MARDUKITE ZUISM DEFINITIONS FOR SYSTEMOLOGY.

<u>ALPHA SPIRIT</u> = a spiritual lifeform; the True Self or "I-AM"; the spirit that is controlling the physical body or "genetic vehicle" using a Lifeline or continuum of spiritual "ZU" energy.

<u>ASCENSION</u> = actualized Awareness elevated to (AN) spiritual existence that is exterior to beta-existence.

BETA-EXISTENCE = manifestation in the Physical Universe (KI); the state of existence or condition of frequency specific to physical energy and physical matter in physical space.

FRAGMENTATION = breaking into parts; fractioning wholeness; fracture of holism; discontinuity; separation; outside the state of Self-Honesty.

GENETIC VEHICLE = a physical life-form; the physical (beta) body controlled by the (Alpha) Spirit using a continuous Lifeline of ZU energy.

HUMAN CONDITION = a default programmed conditioned state standard issue Human existence/experience.

ZU-LINE = a spectrum of Spiritual Life-Energy (ZU); an energetic channel or Identity-Continuum connecting Alpha Spirit Awareness from Infinity-to-Infinity including the full physical beta range.

THE HIGHEST FORM OF TRUE DIVINE WORSHIP.

The true Destiny of Humanity is to achieve spiritual <u>Self-Actualization</u>; the reunion of Self with the Divine. Attaining Self-Honesty in this Life is the most important step a person can take toward achieving their highest ideals, goals and realizations.

The Highest form of "True Worship" begins with the Spirit—the true Self—and all external practices, rituals, ceremonies and historical examples are but outer reflections of this ideal. The Highest form of "Sin" is against the Spirit —against the Self—and its ability to maintain Self-Honesty. There are modes of thought, action and Self-direction of effort that will contribute toward Ascension; and modes that lead away from that.

Beta experiences of "Sin"—pain, fear, guilt, anger—are all related to personal fragmentation; and emotional turbulence from all of these may be released—and intention energy redirected— because: <u>we are all co-creators of Reality in this lifetime!</u>

SPHERES OF EXISTENCE, INFLUENCE & UTILITARIAN ETHICS OF SYSTEMOLOGY.

The prime directive of all beta existence is: *to exist*. The continuation of existence is the purpose behind all existence. Between realization of Self and Infinity, there are many spheres of existence that we may influence. All of the spheres are interconnected.

There is nothing in existence that is in absolute exclusion to all existence. Each sphere of existence supports subsequent existences and assists reaches toward higher spheres of influence.

The greatest good contributes to the greatest continuation of optimum existence for the greatest sphere of inclusion. Degrees of rightness and wrongness are determined by Cosmic Law and are reflected in the quality of, and continuation of, an optimal existence at the highest sphere of existence.

Individual happiness is attained via the channel to the highest sphere. Human unhappiness is the result of "selfishness" and/or lack of "spiritual Self-Actualization" and "Awareness."

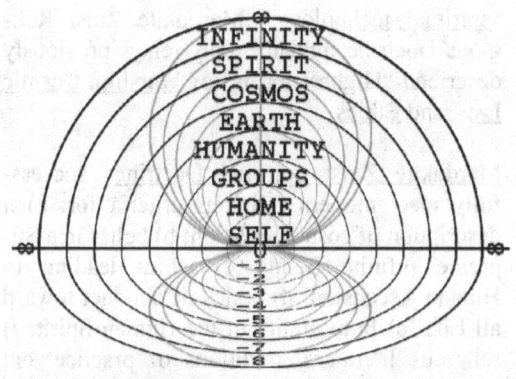

ZU : MARDUKITE ZUISM & MODERN ZUIST RELIGION.

History demonstrates how dangerous, troublesome and easily misused the concept of "RELIGION" is; so, for purposes of incorporating Mardukite Zuism as a contemporary standard, the idea of "religion" is here treated as:

> a concise spiritual paradigm, set of beliefs and practices, regarding Divinity, Infinite Beingness—or else "God."

Mardukite Zuism operates under a premise of very specific beliefs and a "<u>systemology</u>" of "spiritual technology." Mardukite Zuist Religious Doctrine fundamentally relays previously described "Highest forms" of Worship, Cosmic Law, and Ethics.

Mardukite Zuist Spiritual Doctrines successfully meet modern religious criteria for: a) a description of cosmic creation; b) belief in a Supreme Infinite Being; c) ethics leading to Human Ascension; d) ethics of conduct toward all Life; e) Immortality of the Human Spirit; f) religious literature, traditions of practice and spiritual advisement.

GOALS & IDEALS OF MARDUKITE ZUISM.

The word "ZU" meant "knowing" in original Sumerian cuneiform script. Goals and ideals of Zuism reflect this. Mardukite Zuism seeks to assist an individual in reclaiming a realization of the True Self or "I-AM" as the Immortal Spirit, in line with a most ancient directive: to "Know Thyself."

In view of the fact that all modern humans are subjected to technologies depriving them of their freedoms to *be*, *think*, *know* and pursue truth: the goals and ideals of Zuism are to effectively revive and repair these very abilities and certainties of the Individual—as an increase of "Actualized Awareness."

INFINITY, "GOD" & SUPREME BEINGNESS

The Spiritual Philosophy of Zuism is systematized by a Standard Model. It demonstrates Absolute Supreme Beingness associated with the Highest realization of "God" as INFINITY. No thing is Higher or Absolute than the Infinity of Nothing—and reducing Supreme Beingness to any finite personality or character trait is to limit and defile with lesser "words."

The Highest Name of God cannot be conceived
—hence our symbolic use of the Infinity Sign:

∞

...or Sumerian cuneiform word-sign: "ABZU"
—"The Infinite Nothingness and
Source of All ZU."

The Spiritual Universe (AN) is *All-as-One* because it exists as an infinite singularity or stasis:

infinite potential with no gradient or observed motion; which is its own continuity.

The Physical Universe (KI) is *All-as-One* because it is in continuous motion, with all manifest parts working systematically as a continuity of beta-existence.

A "spiritual continuum" or "conduit channel" of ZU—absolute energy from the Spiritual Universe (AN)—links our Awareness levels of "I-AM," "True Self" or Spirit ("Alpha Spirit") with the degrees of motion and variation in the Physical Universe.

This Alpha Spirit or "Soul" is the true Awareness, "I" or "Self" connected to the operation and control of the physical body.

THE TRUE HUMAN ALPHA SPIRIT.

The true Self is the "I" or "Spirit" regardless of its position, degree or level of Awareness. Spirit remains. Whatever "spiritual energy-matter" composes the Alpha Spirit or "soul"—it must occupy this "other space" with its spiritual existence and then project its Awareness and Will onto the Physical Universe (KI) in order to experience the Game we call Life.

This "spiritual energy-matter" that composes all Life (as a Lifeforce with Awareness and Consciousness) goes by many names throughout history—but we find the idea first treated as <u>ZU</u> on cuneiform tablets of Mesopotamia.

On an Identity lifeline of ZU energy, all Alpha Spirits are operating from a Spiritual Universe. We refer to this as the ZU-line on the Standard Model.

ZU is the name given to the spiritual essence of all Life in existence—and Self is a concentrated center or focal point as a ZU-continuum or Identity.

The True Self of an Individual Human is a "spiritual universe cause" of "physical universe effects"—engaging as an immortal Alpha Spirit with a Self-determined Will actualized as an Awareness along the ZU-continuum, extending from Infinity-to-Infinity, through every possible frequency and vibration along the total spectrum of physical and metaphysical existence.

THE SYSTEMOLOGY PRACTICES OF SPIRITUAL ADVISEMENT & COUNSELING SERVICES FOR MARDUKITE ZUISM.

The Mardukite Chamberlains were established in 2009 dedicated to recovery and consolidation of all historical, scriptural & ritual records of ancient Babylon in Mesopotamia. In 2011, a Mardukite faction (International Systemology Society) began to research and develop methods to apply ancient wisdom as a futurist spiritual technology that awakens, unlocks and fully actualizes spiritual potential of the Human Condition.

A systematic approach to spirituality is seen on the Standard Model, where ZU-line frequencies are represented at various degrees: "zero-point" body death; cellular activity and sensory perceptions of a genetic body; bio-chemicals induced by emotion; thoughts and intention transmitted between our Alpha Spirit and the "genetic vehicle"—all the way "up" the scale to a perfected clarity of Self-Actualized Awareness of I-AM as our true "Alpha" state, just below Infinity and Absolute Beingness. Full potential of ZU in Consciousness is only altered from its natural state as a result of personal fragmentation of the Human Condition. This may be restored with spiritual practices.

The Pathway to Self-Honesty is a personal journey and spiritual adventure marked by progressive clearing of spiritual energy channels fragmented by the imprinting and programming accumulated from experiences in our environment—the "debris" that fragments the total actualized experience of Self in Awareness as the Alpha Spirit.

The first and most important step—Before an individual can actualize potentials of the Spirit as Self, they must fully realize: the I-AM Self and the Alpha Spirit are One.

This state of Knowingness is the primary intention of basic spiritual practices found in Mardukite Zuism.

"Systemology" books and advanced training courses are also available to Mardukite Ministers seeking to qualify as specialized clergy, priests, priestess, and systematic processing pilots.

CREED OF MARDUKITE ZUISM.
PRINCIPLES OF BELIEF.*

1.) We believe in an Absolute Beingness, which is Infinite—the ABZU—the All-as-One encompassing Source of All Being, Knowing and Awareness to all Alpha (Spiritual-AN) and Beta (Physical-KI) states of existence.

2.) We believe in a spiritual energy of all Life and Awareness—ZU—in the physical universe (beta) that is an effect of a spiritual (Alpha) cause; a Spirit that is cause. This Spirit—in its Alpha state—is the True Self "I-AM" Individual Identity that many have called the "soul."

3.) We believe that the Human Condition is a genetic vehicle used by a spiritual source (AN) to experience the Finite as physical existence (KI)—that we are Awareness (ZU) projected onto a genetic vehicle—and that while the vehicle/body may perish to physical entropy, the "Alpha Spirit" remains immortal and Self-directed to the extent of its own Actualized Awareness.

---

* First drafted in 2019 by Joshua Free with Kyra Kaos.

4.) We believe that the highest form of worship and spirituality is the actualization and advancement of our "Self" as Spirit in Self-Honesty—and that Self-Honesty is the I-AM Alpha state of Being and Knowing, which is realizable in this lifetime.

5.) We believe that the purpose of all existence is: to exist—and that the prime directive of all spiritual Life is: continued existence of spiritual Life and cocreation of habitable Reality. "Good" and "Moral" actions are evaluated to the extent of this end.

6A.) We believe that no Life exists in exclusion to all other Life—and that the conditions of a habitable Reality extending from Self include:
Home; Community; All Humanity; All Life on Earth; All Life in the Universe; All Spiritual Life; and the Infinite.

6B.) We believe in a continued evolution of Alpha Spirit awareness developed beyond one physical life, and that a Spirit experiences many.

7A.) We believe Mardukite Zuism and its applied systemology is a 21st Century AD synthesis of the 21st Century BC wisdom collected on cuneiform tablets and experienced in ancient Mesopotamia, esp. Babylon.

7B.) This cuneiform library included details concerning: beings called the Anunnaki; ordering of the Cosmos; creation of Humanity; and an entire legacy of systematized traditions.

8.) We believe in the continuation of, and proper communication of, the true legacy of Human history—and the ability of every Human to realize that they are a Free Spirit in a Free Zone of Self-Determinism; and no "evils" can affect intentions if an individual is spiritually Self-Actualized in Self-Honesty.

THE ARCANE KNOWLEDGE FROM MARDUK'S TABLET OF DESTINY.*

1.) As above, so below;
On earth as it is in Heaven
an-bala ki-bala an-ba ki an-ba

2.) What the Mind believes, the Spirit reinforces
da-ga nam-ku-zu dingir-Lamma a bi-ib-gar

3.) When disaster is self-made,
no man can interfere
*nig-ku-lam-ma dingir-ra-na-ka su—
tu-tu nu-ub-zu*

4.) What is given in submission
is a catalyst for defiance
nig-gu-gar-ra nig-gaba-gar-ra

5.) Whoever partners with Truth, creates Life
nig-ge-na-ta a-ba in-da-di nam-ti i-u-tu

---

* Excerpted from *"Tablets of Destiny"* by Joshua Free.

THE OLD TESTAMENT OF
ANUNNAKI
GODS OF THIS UNIVERSE

A collection of the most ancient historical cuneiform records accounting for activities of the Anunnaki and their cosmic ordering of the systems in the Physical Universe—specifically those governing Planet Earth and the Human Condition.

EPIC OF CREATION (ENUMA ELIŠ)*
TABLET I

When in the heights the Heavens had not been named,
And the Earth had not yet been named,
And the primeval ABZU, who birthed them,
And TIAMAT, Ancient One, Mother to them all.
Their waters were as One and no field was formed,
No marsh was to be seen;
When of the gods none had been called into being,
And none bore a name, and no destinies were ordained;
Then were created the celestial gods in the midst of heaven,
LAHMU and LAHAMU were called into being
And the Ages increased.
Then ANSAR and KISAR were created,
And the god ANU then came forth who begot NUDIMMUD.‡
Abounding in all wisdom he had no rival.
Thus the Great Gods were established.
But TIAMAT and ABZU were still in confusion,
Troubled and in disorder.
ABZU was not diminished in might, and TIAMAT roared.
ABZU, the begetter of the great gods,
Cried unto MUMMU, his minister, and said:

---

* Mardukite Catalogue = *Tablet N*
‡ *Nudimmud*—an alternate name for *Enki*.

"MUMMU, thou minister that causes my spirit to rejoice,
Come with me to TIAMAT."
So they went and consulted on a plan with regard to the gods, their sons.
ABZU spoke: "Let me destroy their ways, let there be lamentation, and then let us lie down again in peace."
When TIAMAT heard these words, she raged and cried aloud.
She uttered a curse and unto ABZU she asked: "What then shall we do?"
MUMMU answered giving counsel unto ABZU,
"Come, their way is strong, but you can destroy it;
This day you shall have rest, by night shalt thou lie down in peace."
They banded themselves together
And at the side of TIAMAT they advanced; they were furious;
They devised mischief without resting night and day.
They prepared for battle, fuming and raging;
They joined their forces and made weapons invincible;
She spawned monster-serpents, sharp of tooth, and merciless of fang;
With poison, instead of blood, she filled their bodies.
Fierce monster-vipers she clothed with terror.
With splendor she clothed them, she made them of lofty stature.

Whoever beheld them, terror overcame him,
Their bodies reared up and none could withstand their attack.
She set up vipers and dragons, and the monster LAHAMU.
And hurricanes, and raging hounds, and scorpion-men,
And mighty tempests, and fish-men, and rams;
They bore cruel weapons, without fear of the fight.
Her commands were mighty, none could resist them;
After this fashion she made eleven kinds of monsters.
Among the gods who were her sons,
Inasmuch as he had given her support,
She exalted KINGU; in their midst she raised him to power.
To march before the forces, to lead the host,
To give the battle-signal, to advance to the attack,
To direct the battle, to control the fight,
Unto him she entrusted, saying: "I have uttered thy spell,
In the assembly of the gods I have raised thee to power.
The dominion over all the gods have I entrusted unto him.
Be thou exalted, you are my chosen spouse,
May your name be magnified among all ANUNNAKI."
She gave him the Tablets of Destiny, lain them on his breast,

Saying: "Thy command shall not be in vain,
And your decrees shall be established."
Now KINGU, exalted, having received the power of ANU,
Decreed the fate among the gods his sons,
Saying: "Let the opening of your mouth quench the Fire-god;
He who is exalted in the battle, let him display his might!"

EPIC OF CREATION (ENUMA ELIŠ)[*]
TABLET II

TIAMAT made weighty her handiwork,
Evil she wrought against the gods her children.
To avenge ABZU, TIAMAT planned evil,
She had collected her forces, the god unto ENKI[‡] divulged.
ENKI was grievously afflicted and he sat in sorrow.
The days went by, and his anger was appeased,
And to the place of ANSAR his father he took his way.
He went and, standing before ANSAR, his father,
All that TIAMAT had plotted he repeated unto him,
Saying "TIAMAT, our mother has conceived a

---

[*] Mardukite Catalogue = *Tablet N*
[‡] *Enki*—alternate name for him appears as "*E.A.*" in some versions.

hatred for us,
With all her force she rages, full of wrath.
All the gods have turned to her,
With those, whom you created, they go to her side.
They have banded together and at the side of TIAMAT
And they advance; they are furious,
They devise mischief without resting night and day.
They prepare for battle, fuming and raging;
They have joined their forces and are making war.
TIAMAT, who formed all things,
And made weapons invincible;
She has spawned monster-serpents,
Sharp of tooth, and merciless of fang.
With poison, instead of blood, she has filled their bodies.
Fierce monster-vipers she has clothed with terror,
With splendor she has armed them;
She has made them tall in stature.
Whoever beholds them is overcome by terror,
Their bodies rear up and none can withstand their attack.
She has set up vipers, dragons, and the monster LAHAMU,
And hurricanes and raging hounds, and scorpion-men,
And mighty tempests, and fish-men and rams;
They bear cruel weapons, without fear of the fight.
Her commands are mighty; none can resist them;
After this fashion, huge of stature,

She has made eleven kinds of monsters.
Among the gods who are her sons,
Inasmuch as he has given her support,
She has exalted KINGU;
In their midst she has raised him to power.
To march before the forces, to lead the host,
To give the battle-signal, to advance to the attack.
To direct the battle, to control the fight,
To him she has uttered your spell;
She has given to him the Tablets of Destiny,
On his breast she laid hem,
Saying: 'Thy command shall not be in vain,
And the your word shall be established.'
"O my father, let not the word of thy lips be over come,
Let me go, that I may accomplish all that is in thy heart. I shall avenge."

EPIC OF CREATION (ENUMA ELIŠ)*
TABLET III

ANSAR spoke to his minister:
"O GAGA, thou minister who causes my spirit to rejoice,
Unto LAHMU and LAHAMU I will send thee.
Make ready for a feast, at a banquet let them sit,
Let them eat bread, let them mix wine,
That for MARDUK, the avenger, they may decree the fate.

---

* Mardukite Catalogue = *Tablet N*

Go, GAGA, stand before them, And all that I tell thee,
Repeat unto them, and say: 'ANSAR, your son, has sent me,
The purpose of his heart he has made known unto me.
He said TIAMAT, our mother, has conceived a hatred for us,
With all her force she rages full of wrath.
All the gods have turned to her, with those, whom you created,
They go to her side.
I sent ANU, but he could not withstand her;
NUDIMMUD [ENKI] was afraid and turned back.
But MARDUK has set out, champion of the gods, your son;
To set out against TIAMAT his heart has called him.
He opened his mouth and spake unto me, saying
Saying: 'If I, your avenger, Conquer TIAMAT and give you life,
Appoint an assembly, make my fate preeminent and proclaim it so.
In UPSUKKINAKU seat yourself joyfully together;
With my word in place I will decree fate.
May whatsoever I do remain unaltered,
May the word of my lips never be changed nor made of no avail.'
Quickly decree for him the fate which you bestow
So that he may go and fight your strong enemy."

GAGA went humbly before LAHMU and
  LAHAMU, the gods,
His fathers, and he kissed the ground at their feet.
He humbled himself; then he stood up and spake
  unto them saying:
"ANSAR, your son, has sent me,
The purpose of his heart he has made known unto
  me.
He says that TIAMAT, our mother, has conceived
  a hatred for us,
With all her force she rages full of wrath."
And he spoke the words of the tale.
LAHMU and LAHAMU heard and cried aloud.
All of the IGIGI wailed bitterly, saying:
"We do not understand the deed of TIAMAT!"
Then did they collect and go,
The great gods, all of them, the ANUNNAKI who
  decree fate.
They entered in the House of ANSAR, kissed one
  another,
They made ready for the feast, ate bread,
And they mixed sesame-wine.
They were wholly at ease, their spirit was exalted;
Then for MARDUK, their avenger, they decreed
  the fate.

EPIC OF CREATION (ENUMA ELIŠ)[*]
TABLET IV

The ANUNNAKI prepared for MARDUK a lordly chamber,
Before his fathers as prince he took his place.
"MARDUK, You are now chief among the great gods,
Thy fate is unequaled, thy word is ANU.[‡]
Your words shall be command,
In your power shall it be to exalt and to abase.
None among the gods shall transgress your boundary.
Abundance, shall exist in thy sanctuary shrine,
Even if you lack offerings.
MARDUK, you are our avenger!
We give you sovereignty over the whole world.
Sit down in might; be exalted in thy command.
Your weapon shall never lose power; it shall crush your enemy.
Lord, spare the life of him that puts his trust in thee,
But as for the god who began the rebellion, empty them of life."
The ANUNNAKI set out a garment
And continued to speak to MARDUK.
"May thy fate, lord, be supreme among the gods,

---

[*] Mardukite Catalogue = *Tablet N*

[‡] "...thy word is *Anu*"—given as "thy word is *Enlil*" in some versions.

To destroy and to create; speak only the word,
And your command shall be fulfilled.
Command now that the garment vanish;
And speak the word again and let the garment reappear!"
Then he spake the words and the garment vanished;
Again he commanded it and the garment reappeared.
When the gods, his fathers, beheld the fulfillment of his word,
They rejoiced, and they did homage unto him,
Saying, "Maerdechai! Maerdechai! MARDUK is king!"
They bestowed upon him the scepter, the throne and the ring,
They give him invincible weaponry to overwhelm the enemy.
"Go, and cut off the life of TIAMAT," they said.
"And let the wind carry her blood into secret places."
MARDUK made ready the bow, his first choice in weapon,
He slung a spear upon him.
He raised the club in his right hand.
The bow and the quiver he hung at his side.
He set the FLAMING DISC in front of him
And with the flame he filled his body.
He fashioned a net to enclose the inward parts of TIAMAT,
He stationed the four winds so that nothing of her

might escape;
The South wind and the North wind and the East wind,
And the West wind He created the evil wind,
And the tempest, and the hurricane,
And the fourfold wind,
And the sevenfold wind, and the cyclone,
And the wind which had no equal;
He sent forth the winds which he had created, seven in total;
To disturb the inward parts of TIAMAT.
Then MARDUK raised the thunderbolt, mounted the chariot,
A storm unequaled for terror, and he harnessed four horses
Named DESTRUCTION, FEROCITY, TERROR,
And SWIFTNESS; and foam came from their mouths
And they were mighty in battle,
Trained to trample underfoot.
With garments cloaked in terror and an overpowering brightness
Crowning his head, MARDUK set out toward the raging TIAMAT.
Then the gods beheld him.
And when the lord drew near,
He gazed upon the inward parts of TIAMAT,
He heard the muttering of KINGU, her spouse.
As MARDUK gazed, KINGU was troubled,
The will of KINGU was destroyed and his motions ceased.

And the gods, his helpers, who marched by his side,
Beheld their leader's fear and their sight was troubled.
But TIAMAT did not turn her neck.
She spit rebellious words.
MARDUK raised the thunderbolt,
His mighty weapon, against TIAMAT,
Who was raging, and he called out:
"You have become great as you have exalted your self on high,
And your heart has prompted you to call to battle.
You have raised KINGU to be your spouse,
You have chosen Evil and sinned against ANU and his decree.
And against the gods, my fathers,
You have dedicated yourself to a wicked plan.
Let us face off now then in battle!"
When TIAMAT heard these words,
She acted possessed and lost her sense of reason.
She screamed wild, piercing cries,
She trembled and shook to her very foundations.
She recited an incantation, and cast a spell,
And the gods of the battle cried out for their weapons.
Then TIAMAT and MARDUK advanced towards one another,
The battle drew near.
Lord MARDUK spread out his net and caught her,
And the evil wind that gathered behind him he let loose in her

Face when she opened her mouth fully.
The terrible winds filled her belly,
And her courage was taken from her,
And her mouth opened wider.
MARDUK seized the spear and burst her belly,
Severing her inward parts, he pierced her heart.
He overcame her and cut off her life;
He cast down her body and stood upon it.
After slaying TIAMAT, the leader of the
　ANCIENT ONES,
The might was broken and her minions scattered.
But they were surrounded, so that they could not
　escape.
MARDUK took them captive and broke their
　weapons;
In the net they were caught and in the snare they
　sat down.
And on the eleven monsters which she had filled
With the power of striking terror, he brought them
　affliction,
Their strength he stole and their opposition
He trampled under his feet.
From KINGU who he had conquered,
He rightly took the Tablets of Destiny
And sealed them with his seal, then hung them
　from his neck.
Now after MARDUK had conquered and cast
　down his enemies,
And had fully established ANSAR's triumph over
　the enemy,

And had attained the purpose of NUDUMMID,[*]
Over the captive gods he strengthened his position,
And he returned to the conquered TIAMAT.
With his merciless club he smashed her skull.
He cut through the channels of her blood,
And he made the North wind steal it away
Outside in secret places between spaces.
His fathers beheld, and rejoiced and were glad;
Presents and gifts they brought unto him.
Then Lord MARDUK rested, gazing upon her dead body
And devised a cunning plan.
He split her up like a flat fish into two halves;
One half of her he established a covering for heaven.
Sealed with a GATE he stationed a WATCHER IAK SAKKAK
And fixed him not to let her waters to ever come forth.
MARDUK passed through and surveyed the regions of Heaven,
And over the Deep he set the dwelling of E.A. [ENKI].
And after measuring the structure of the Deep,
He founded his Mansion,
Which was created likened to Heaven and he set down
The fixed districts for ANU, ENLIL and ENKI to reign.

---

[*] E.A. (Enki)

EPIC OF CREATION (ENUMA ELIŠ)[*]
TABLET V

MARDUK fixed the Star Gates of the Elder Gods;[‡]
And the stars he gave images as the stars of the Zodiac, which he fixed in place.
He ordained the year and into sections he divided it;
For the twelve months he fixed the stars.
He founded his Star Gate on NIBIRU[†] to fix them in zones;
That none might rebel or go astray,
He fixed the Star Gate of ENLIL[∞]
And IA [ENKI] alongside him.
He opened great gates on both sides,
He made strong gates on the left and on the right
And in the midst thereof he fixed the zenith;
He fixed the Star Gate for the Moon-god
And decreed that he shine forth,
Trusting him with the night and to determine days;
The first of the great gates he assigned to NANNA [called SIN]
And every month without ceasing he would be

---

[*] Mardukite Catalogue = *Tablet N*
[‡] Presumably the formation (cosmic ordering) of the local universe (solar system).
[†] Alt. "*Nebiru*"—which some have interpreted as the planet Jupiter.
[∞] Many Chaldeo-Babylonian sources list as "*Gate of Bel.*"

crowned,
Saying: "At the beginning of the month, when you shine down upon the land,
You command the trumpets of the six days of the moon,
And on the seventh day you will divide the crown.
On the fourteenth day you will stand opposite as half-moon.
When the Sun-god of the foundation of heaven calls thee,
On that the final day again you will stand as opposite.
All shall go about the course I fix.
You will drawn near to judge the righteous
And destroy the unrighteous.
That is my decree and the covenant of the first gate."
The gods, his fathers, beheld the net which MARDUK had fashioned,
They beheld his bow and how its work was accomplished.
They praised the work which he had done and then ANU raised up
And kissed the bow before the assembly of the gods.
And thus he named the names of the bow, saying:
"Long-wood shall be one name,
And the second name shall be Dragonslayer,
And its third name shall be the Bow-star,
In heaven shall it remain as a sign to all."
ANU and MARDUK fixed a Star Gate for it too,

And after the ANUNNAKI decreed the fates for
   the ANCIENT ONES,
MARDUK set a throne in heaven for himself at
   ANU's right hand.

EPIC OF CREATION (ENUMA ELIŠ)*
TABLET VI

The ANUNNAKI acclaimed him "First among the
   ELDER GODS."
MARDUK heard the praises of the gods,
His heart called to him to devised a cunning plan.
He approached IA [ENKI] saying:
"The Key to the GATE shall be ever hidden,
   except to my offspring.
I will take my blood and with bone I will fashion a
   Race of Men,
That they may keep watch over the GATE.
And from the blood of KINGU I will create a race
   of men,
That they will inhabit the Earth in service to the
   gods
So that our shrines may be built and the temples
   filled.
But I will alter the ways of the gods, and I will
   change their paths;
Together shall they be oppressed
And unto evil shall they no longer reign.
I will bind the ELDER GODS to the

---

*   Mardukite Catalogue = *Tablet N*

WATCHTOWERS,
Let them keep watch over the GATE of ABSU,
And the GATE of TIAMAT and the GATE of KINGU.
I bind the WATCHER IAK SAKKAK to the GATE
With the Key known only to my Race.
Let none enter that GATE
Since to invoke DEATH is to utter the final prayer."
The ANUNNAKI rejoiced and set their mansions in UPSUKKINAKU.
When all this had been done, the Elders of the ANUNNAKI
Seated themselves around MARDUK
And in their assembly they exalted him
And named him FIFTY times,
Bestowing upon him the FIFTY powers of the gods.

EPIC OF CREATION (ENUMA ELIŠ) TABLET VII – THE FIFTY NAMES*

1. The First Name is MARDUK-DUGGA-ANU, Son of the Sun, Lord of Lords, Master of Magicians, Most Radiant Among the Gods is he.

2. The Second Name is MARDUKKA, ANUNNAKI Creator, Knower of the Secrets of MARDUK, Time, Space & Creation.

---

* Mardukite Catalogue = *Tablet F*

3. The Third Name is ARRA-MARUTUKKU, Master of Protections and of the Gate to the ANCIENT ONES, And to whom the people give praise as Protector of the City. Possesses the ARRA-Star.

4. The Fourth Name is BARASHAK-USHU-BAALDURU, Worker of Miracles, with wide heart and strong sympathies.

5. The Fifth Name is LUGGAL-DIMMERANKI-BANU-TUKKU, Commander of the Wind Demons, The Voice Heard Among the Gods.

6. The Sixth Name is NARI-LUGGAL-DIMMERANKI(A)-BAN-RABISHU, Watcher of the Star Gates of the IGIGI & ANUNNAKI, And who is named the Monitor of the Gods in their stations. Keeper of the Gates between worlds.

7. The Seventh Name is ASARU-LU-DU-BAN-MASKIM, Wielder of the Flaming Sword, The Light of the Gods. Called for the safety and protection of the Gatekeeper.

8. The Eighth Name is NAMTIL-LAKU-BAN-UTUK-UKUT-UKKU, Master of the Death Gate and of Necromancy, And who is able to revive the Gods with a single prayer.

9. The Ninth Name is NAMRU-BAKA-KALAMU, The Shining One who is Counselor of the Sciences. Called to increase the scientific knowledge of the Gatekeeper.

10. The Tenth Name is ASARU-BAALPRIKU, Creator of grains and plants, who knows no wasteland. Called to increase the vegetative and blooming growth.

11. The Eleventh Name is ASARU-ALIM-BAR-MARATU, Who is revered for wisdom in the house of counsel, And who is looked to for peace when the Gods are unsettled. Called to aid in communication with the ANUNNAKI and to dispel deception.

12. The Twelfth Name is ASARU-ALIM-NUNA-BANA-TATU, The Mighty One who is the Light of the Father of the Gods, And who directs the decrees of ANU, ENLIL and ENKI/EA. Called to aid in the enforcement of law on Earth.

13. The Thirteenth Name is (NABU)-TUTU, He who created them anew, and should their wants be pure, then they are satisfied. Called to reveal the hidden gnosis within the Gatekeeper.

14. The Fourteenth Name is ZI-UKKINA-GIBIL-ANU, The life of the Assembly of the Gods Who established for a bright place for the Gods in the heavens. Called to reveal secrets of astrology and the celestial sphere.

15. The Fifteenth Name is ZI-AZAG-ZI-KU-IGIGI-MAGAN-PA, Bringer of Purification, God

of the Favoring Breeze, Carrier of Wealth & Abundance to the people.

16. The Sixteenth Name is AGAKU-AZAG-MASH-GARZANNA, Lord of the Pure Incantation, The Merciful One, And whose name is on the mouth of the Created Race. Called to bring life to wards and elementary spirits.

17. The Seventeenth Name is TUKUMU-AZAG-MASH-SHAMMASHTI, Knower of the Incantation to destroy all evil ones. Called in the Maqlu Rite to dispel evil sorceries.

18. The Eighteenth Name is SAHG-ZU-MASH-SHANANNA, Founder of the Assembly of Gods and knows their heart, And whose name is heralded among the IGIGI. Called for aiding the Gatekeepers psychic development.

19. The Nineteenth Name is ZI-SI-MASH-IN-ANNA, Reconciler of enemies, who puts an end to anger; the Bringer of Peace.

20. The Twentieth Name is SUH-RIM-MASH-SHA-NERGAL, Destroyer of wicked foes, who confuses their plans. May be sent to destroy the enemies of the Gatekeeper.

21. The Twenty-first Name is SUH-KUR-RIM-MASH-SHADAR, Who confounds the wicked foes in their places. May be sent to destroy unknown enemies of the Gatekeeper.

22. The Twenty-second Name is ZAH-RIM-MASH-SHAG-ARANNU, Lord of Lightning, A warrior among warriors. May be raised against entire armies of men.

23. The Twenty-third Name is ZAH-KUR-RIM-MASH-TI-SHADDU, Destroyer of the Enemy in battle, Who slays in a most unnatural fashion.

24. The Twenty-fourth Name is ENBILULU-MASH-SHA-NEBU, Knower of the secrets of water and of secret places for grazing. Called to bestow the secrets of dowsing and aid irrigation.

25. The Twenty-fifth Name is EPADUN-E-YUNGINA-KANPA, Lord of Irrigation, who sprinkles the waters in the heavens and on Earth. As the previous; also the secrets of Sacred Geometry.

26. The Twenty-sixth Name is ENBI-LULU-GUGAL-AGGA, Lord of growth and cultivation, who raises grains to maturity, And some have said is a face of ENKI.

27. The Twenty-seventh Name is HEGAL-BURDISHU, Master of farming and the plentiful harvest And who provides for the people's consumption. May also be called to aid in personal fertility.

28. The Twenty-eighth Name is SIRSIR-APIRI-KUBAB-ADAZU-ZU-KANPA, The domination of TIAMAT by the power of the Net. Called for mastery of the Serpent and the Kundalini.

29. The Twenty-ninth Name is MAL-AHK-BACH-ACHA-DUGGA, Lord of bravery and courage, Rider of the Ancient Worm. Summoned for courage, bravery and self-confidence.

30. The Thirtieth Name is GIL-AGGA-BAAL, Furnisher of the life-giving seed, Beloved (betrothed) consort to INANNA-ISHTAR. Called for women who desire pregnancy.

31. The Thirty-first Name is GILMA-AKKA-BAAL, Mighty One and Divine Architect of the temples. Possesses secrets concerning the Geometry of the Universe.

32. The Thirty-second Name is AGILMA-MASH-SHAY-E-GURRA, Maker of Rain Clouds to nourish the fields of the Earth. Called forth in times of drought.

33. The Thirty-third Name is ZULUM-MU-AB-BA-BAAL, Giver of excellent counsel and power in all businesses, And Destroyer of the wicked foe, maintaining goodness and order.

34. The Thirty-fourth Name is MUMMU, Creator of the Universe from the flesh of TIAMAT. Keeper of the Four Watchtower Gates to the Outside.

35. The Thirty-fifth Name is ZU-MUL-IL-MAR-AN-DARA-BAAL, The heavens have none equal in strength and vitality. Called forth to aid in healing rituals and rites.

36. The Thirty-sixth Name is AGISKUL-AG-NI-BAAL-LUGAL-ABDUBAR, Who sealed the ANCIENT ONES in the abyss. Called by the piously righteous for strength and vigor.

37. The Thirty-seventh Name is PAGALGUEN-NA-ARRA-BA-BAAL, Possessor of Infinite Intelligence, preeminent among the Gods. Offers wisdom in oracles and divination.

38. The Thirty-eighth Name is LUGAL-DURMAH-ARATA-AGAR-BAAL, King of the gods, Lord of Rulers [Durmah]. Aids the Gatekeeper in developing all mystic powers.

39. The Thirty-ninth Name is ARA-ADU-NUNA-ARAMAN-GI, Counselor of ENKI [EA], who created the Gods, his fathers, And whose princely ways are no other God can equal. Called during (self)-initiations to aid you through the Gates.

40. The Fortieth Name is DUL-AZAG-DU-MU-DUKU-ARATA-GIGI, Possessor the secret knowledge and the wand of Lapis Lazuli. Can reveal untold marvels of the cosmos to the Gatekeeper.

41. The Forty-first Name is LUGAL-ABBA-

BAAL-DIKU, Eldest of the Elder Ones, and pure is his dwelling among them. Aids the Gatekeeper in acquiring "self-honesty."

42. The Forty-second Name is LUGAL-DUL-AZAGA-ZI-KUR, Knower of the secrets of the spirits of wind and star. Offers the Gatekeeper secrets to command the spirits.

43. The Forty-third Name is IR-KINGU-BAR-E-RIMU, Holding the capture of KINGU, supreme is his might. Keeper of the Blood(Birth)-Rights.

44. The Forty-fourth Name is KI-EN-MA-EN-GAIGAI, Supreme Judge of the ANUNNAKI, at whose name the gods quake. To be called when no other spirit will arrive.

45. The Forty-fifth Name is E-ZIS-KUR-NENIGEGAI, Knows the lifespan of all things, And who fixed the Created Race's life at 120 years.

46. The Forty-sixth Name is GIBIL-GIRRA-BAAL-AGNI-TARRA, Lord of the sacred fire and the forge, creator of the Sword. Also possesses the secrets of the "fiery passions."

47. The Forty-seventh Name is ADDU-KAKO-DAMMU, Raiser of storms that blanket the skies of Heaven.

48. The Forty-eighth Name is ASH-ARRU-BAX-

TAN-DABAL, Keeper of time, the secrets of the past and future. May be summoned to aid acts of divination.

49. The Forty-ninth Name is The Star, Let NEBIRU be his name, He who forced his way through the midst of TIAMAT, May he hold the ALPHA and the OMEGA in his hands. Summoned to discern the Destiny of the Universe.

50. The Fiftieth Name is FIFTY and NINNU-AM-GASHDIG, The Judge of Judges, Determiner of the laws of the Realm. The Patron of the Dragonblood Kings of Earth.

EPIC OF CREATION (ENUMA ELIŠ)
THE MARDUK TABLET APOCRYPHA[*]

The Forty-ninth Name is the STAR, that which shines in the heavens.
May he hold the ALPHA and the OMEGA in his hands,
And may all pay homage unto him, saying:
"He who forced his way through the midst of TIAMAT without resting,
Let NIBIRU[‡] be his name—"The Seizer of the Crossings"
That causes stars of heaven to uphold their paths.

---

[*] Mardukite Catalogue = *Tablet F*
[‡] Alt. "*Nebiru*"—"crossings" as in "midsection" or "midway around."

He comes as a shepherd to the gods who are like
  sheep.
In the future of mankind at the End of Days,
May this be heard without ceasing; may it hold
  sway forever!
Since MARDUK has created the realm of heaven
  and fashioned the firm earth,
He is forever the Lord of this World."
ENLIL listened. ENKI heard and rejoiced.
All of the Spirits of Heaven waited.
ENLIL gave to MARDUK his name and title BEL.
ENKI gave to MARDUK his name and title EA
  and said:
"The binding of all my decrees, let MARDUK
  now control.
All of my commands, shall he make known."
The Fiftieth Name is FIFTY and NINNU-AM-
  GASHDIG,
The Judger of Judges, Determiner of the laws of
  the Realm.
By the name FIFTY did the ANUNNAKI then
  proclaim MARDUK's "Fifty Names."
The ANUNNAKI made his path preeminent.
Let all hold remebrance of the Fifty Names of
  MARDUK;
And let the leaders proclaim them;
Let the wise gather to consider them together,
Let the father repeat them and teach them to his
  son;
Let them be in the ears of the priest and the
  shepherd.

Let all rejoice in MARDUK, the Lord of the gods,
That be may cause the land, his Earth, to be
  prosperous,
And that he himself may enjoy prosperity!
His word hold and his command is unaltered;
No utterance from his mouth goes unnoticed.
His gaze is of anger and turns his back to none;
No god can withstand his wrath.
And yet, wide is his heart and broad is his
  compassion;
The sinner and evil-doer in his presence weep for
  themselves
And pray for forgiveness.

KINGSHIP OF THE ANCIENT ONES[*]

Formerly, in the Ancient of Days,
ALULU[‡] reigned in Heaven,
And for nine sars did he rule the skies,
But he did not reign well.
Then in the ninth sar of his reign,
ANU attacked and defeated ALULU.
ALULU then descended from Heaven
And ruled the dark-hued Earth.
By the decree of ANU,
Kingship was lowered from Heaven to Earth
Then ANU gave fight and defeated ALULU
  on Earth.

---

[*] Mardukite Catalogue = *Tablet K*
[‡] Alt. "*Alalu*"—appears in some tablets regarding
Kingship in "Heaven."

THE RISE OF THE GODS OF EARTH*

When first the gods were men on Earth
Settling on the Bond of Heaven-Earth,
ANU decreed that the ANUNNAKI would come forth.
They were forced to toil and do labor.
Great indeed was the drudgery of the gods,
The labor was heavy the misery not befitting of gods:
And the Seven Great ANUNNAKI were not free of the burden
And the IGIGI‡ were called down to do physical labor.
And these "giants" roamed the Earth in a time before men.
Because the grain-goddess had not arrived,
Because the cattle-goddess had not been born,
There was no cattle and there was no grain.
The ANUNNAKI were forced to eat plants like sheep
And drink water from the ditches.
They dug rivers and opened canals to be the life of the land.
The IGIGI also dug rivers and opened canals.
Then the IGIGI dug the Tigris river and the Euphrates.

---

* Mardukite Catalogue = *Tablet A*
‡ *Igigi*—from the cuneiform "*igi*" meaning "see" or "eye" that is compounded "*igi-igi*" as "(over)seers" "those that see" or "watchers."

From the depths of Earth they brought forth
springs of water.
And the wells of life they established.
They gathered up earth to build up all the
   mountains.
And for years they toiled under such drudgery.
And they had counted the years of their labors,
For ten cycles they suffered the toil night and day.
For twenty cycles they suffered toil night and day.
For thirty cycles they suffered the toil night and
   day.
For forty cycles too much had they toiled night
   and day.
Elder Gods of the ANUNNAKI came together.
With lots they decided the fate of the Earth.
To ANU the Father of the Heavens, would remain
   in Heaven.
To ENLIL, Royal Heir was given the Command.
To EA [ENKI], was given control of the Waters of
   Life.
But in the lands, only endless toiling transpired.
In the ditches, the IGIGI began murmuring against
   the work.
"Let us confront our foremen," they declared.
He must take off our heavy burden upon us!
Let us confront ENLIL, the Commander of the
   ANUNNAKI.
Come, let us go to him and pull him from his
   E.KUR."‡

---

‡ *E.Kur*—in Sumerian, "House like a mountain"; the

So the IGIGI set their tools on fire,
Picked themselves up and moved to the Gate of ENLIL.
It was nighttime when the E.KUR was surrounded,
But ENLIL was not aware of their advances.
The IGIGI approached the Gate of ENLIL
NUSKU opened up his Gate to the E.KUR,
And he took his weapons in as he stood.
ENLIL gathered with the Assembly of the ANUNNAKI,
At the Gate, the Gatekeeper spoke out to those gathered:
"Now, then, ANU, your Father in Heaven,
And also your counselor and General of the Armies, ENLIL,
And your prefect goddess queen, NINURTA,
And ENKI, Lord on Earth, has commanded me to ask you:
Who is the initiator of this battle?
Who is the initiator of these hostilities toward this place?
Who has declared a war, and brought war upon the Gate of ENLIL?"
The IGIGI [Watchers] shouted out:
"Everyone of us among the IGIGI has declared war;
We take our stand now against the endless excavations of land,
And excessive toils and slave labor has killed us,

---

official ziggurat sanctuary of Enlil "when on Earth."

Our forced drudgery has been too heavy, the
  misery too much!
Now, everyone of us IGIGI has resolved that a
new covenant shall be made with ENLIL."
A grand Assembly of ANUNNAKI was advised.
A message was sent to ANU to come down from
  the heavens.
The Lord ENKI was brought to their presence
And the resolution came from ENKI.
To relieve the misery of the IGIGI,
The fateful decision was made:
A race of humans would be created to be the new
  Workers...

CREATION OF THE HUMAN FORM (THE ADAMU)*

On the eve of the Great Rebellion of the IGIGI
  [Watchers],
EA [ENKI] made ready to speak out,
And EA [ENKI] said to the ANUNNAKI, his
  brothers:
"What can we really say about their claims?
Their forced labor has been heavy and their misery
  is too much.
Every day the younger gods [IGIGI] toil endlessly,
And the outcry has been made loud, we could all
  hear the clamor.
There is another way: The fashioning of a

---
* Mardukite Catalogue = *Tablet G*

Primitive Worker [LULU AMELU].
NIN-HAR-SAG [MAMMI], the midwife of the ANUNNAKI, is present.
Come, let us ask her to create a human, a man, in our likeness,
And let him bear the endless toils; let him bear the slaved labor.
Let the humans assume the drudgery of the gods."
Together, they summoned and asked the birth-goddess,
The midwife of the ANUNNAKI, wise MAMMI:
"Will you be the birth-goddess for the creatures of mankind?
If you create a human being, that he can bear the toil of the gods,
Let him bear the work and tasks of ENLIL‡
And let man assume the drudgery of the gods."
The Lady of Life [NINHURSAG/MAMMI now called NINTI]
Made reply to the Assembly of ANUNNAKI:
"The task is not for me, but for ENKI.
It is ENKI who commands the purification and the Waters of Life,
If ENKI will provide for me the clay, then I will make the creation."
ENKI listened and made ready his reply in the ANUNNAKI Assembly:
"On the first, seventh, and fifteenth days of the month,

---

‡ *Enki* in some versions.

I will establish the purification bath.
First, let one god be sacrificed and the rest cleansed by baptism.
Let NINTI mix the clay with his [the sacrificed god] flesh and blood.
And let us hear the the sound of drums for the rest of the time.
From the flesh of the god let a spirit remain until the End of Days,
And let it be known to the living gods by the sign marked,
Or else he will be allowed to be forgotten, so let the spirit remain."
From the great Assembly of the ANUNNAKI was heard a unanimous: "Yes!"
On the first, seventh, and fifteenth days of the month,
ENKI established the purification bath.
They bled the god AWMELU, before the Assembly of ANUNNAKI.
NINTI mixed clay with the flesh and blood of AWMELU.
That same god and man were thoroughly mixed in the clay,
To the ADAMU they sought to bestow the face of the gods.
For the remainder of the period they heard the drum beat.
From the flesh of the god the spirit remained to the End of Days.
It was made known to the living gods by the sign

marked,
Without which he be allowed to be forgotten, so the spirit remained.
And after she had mixed the clay,
She summoned forth the great gods [ANUNNAKI] and the IGIGI [Watchers]
Who each in turn 'spat' upon the clay.
MAMMI [changed from NINTU now] spoke before the gods:
"You have ordered me a task and I have completed it.
You have sacrificed the god and his 'Divine Spark'
And I have done away with your heavy slave labor,
Whereby I have imposed the drudgery of the gods on man.
You have bestowed troubles upon mankind for all Eternity.
I have released the yoke from you and given it to my creation,
I have made restoration of the peace among gods."
When they heard her speak these words,
They ran carefree to her side and kissed her feet, saying:
"Formerly we have given to you the name MAMMI
But now let your name be Mistress of all the Gods!"
When mankind came forth, it knew nothing of eating bread,
Knew nothing of dressing in garments,

They ate plants with beasts of the field and drank in water holes used by animals.
He became possessed with intelligence but grew wild.
Hybrid in nature, unable to reproduce alone.
NINGISHZIDDA‡ came forthright,
Two branches were added to Man's Tree of Life,
The tortuous serpent therein residing, and a perfect ADAMU had come forth.
And the ADAMU proliferated on the Earth.
For seven cycles were they were forced to work in ABZU
Before ENKI created the Edaphic Line by ADAPA.

WISE ONE AMONG HUMANS (ADAPA)*

Taking the role of ANU upon himself,
ENKI did procreate with an Earthling female,
Not DAMKINA the goddess, but with an Earthling female
Did ENKI cause a child to be born: ADAPA.
ENKI gave to him a wide ear to be granted wisdom.
Secrets of ANU, ENLIL and ENKI did he pass on to ADAPA.
He gave to him Secrets of the Divine Tablets of Destiny,

---

‡ *Ningishzida*—meaning "Lord of the Tree of Life" presumably DNA.
* Mardukite Catalogue = *Tablet G*

But he did not grant him eternal life.
ADAPA was raised in those days as a wise man in ERIDU.
ENKI had created him to be a chief among men,
The wisest of men whose command none could oppose.
Very prudent, and wise with the knowledge of the ANUNNAKI was he.
Without blame, with hands who had not yet toiled, an anointed one,
Shown the secrets of the oil and water,
The means of observing the divine statutes was shown ADAPA.
With the bakers of ERIDU, he baked bread—
The food and the water for ERIDU he helped prepare daily,
And with his pure hands he prepared the table,
And without him the table was not cleared.
To sail he was taught and fishing and hunting—for ERIDU he did well.
Attending to ENKI, servant of the king in his chamber upon the bed.
At the end of each day, the closing preparations of ERIDU he attended to.
Upon the pure new moon ADAPA had set his ship upon a journey.
But the winds were blowing when his ship departed the shore.
Taking the oar, he navigated his ship upon the broad sea,
And the wings of the South Wind beat against the

air so badly
He had been driven back to the House of ENKI, and said:
"South Wind, on the way across the sea you beat your wings
And I shall set a curse against everything that that opposes my journey.
Your wing, I will break." He spoke the words.
The wing of the South Wind was broken,
For seven days the South Wind did not blow upon the land.
ANU called forth his messenger and asked:
"Why has the South Wind not blown upon the land for seven days?"
His messenger answered him: "My lord ANU, ADAPA, the son of ENKI,
Has broken the wing of the South Wind."
When ANU heard these words, he yelled: "What? What!"
ANU ascended from his throne before the Assembly of ANUNNAKI,
"I command that someone bring him here before me for inspection."
ADAPA, more intelligent than the ADAMU, was roused.
ADAPA, King of All Men, ENKI roused from sleep.
ENKI was wise with the ways of Heaven and Earth,
And ENKI sought to prepare ADAPA for the journey.

With the vestments of mourning ADAPA was clothed.
With wisdom of Heaven, ENKI imparted knowledge to ADAPA:
"My son you have been commanded to go to Heaven
To stand before the face of ANU in the Assembly of the ANUNNAKI.
When you rise upon the plane you will approach the Gate of ANU,
The Gate of ANU is guarded by DAMMUZ and NINGISHZIDDA.
When they see you they will ask who you are and why you are there,
They will ask why you wear the vestments of mourning,
For which you will reply that two gods have vanished from your country,
And when they ask what two gods, who in the land has vanished,
Give to them the names: DAMMUZ and NINGISHZIDDA.
They will look at one another bewildered and be astonished.
They will speak to ANU of your arrival and show you the way to him.
Food of Death they will set before you in the Assembly of the ANUNNAKI,
Do not eat it, for to eat with the gods is to die.
Water of death they will set before you in the Assembly of the ANUNNAKI,

Do not drink it, for to drink with the gods is to die.
The vestments that they set before you, dress yourself in them.
The oil that they set before you, anoint yourself with it.
This is the counsel I would give to you, Child of ENKI. Forget nothing."
In short time, the messenger of Anu came to the House of ENKI:
"Adapa has broken the wing of the South Wind.
ANU commands that he be brought before him in Heaven."
The road to Heaven was shown to ADAPA and to Heaven he was raised.
When he came to Heaven and approached the Gate of ANU,
The Gate of ANU was guarded by DAMMUZ and NINGISHZIDDA.
When they saw ADAPA approach, they cried:
"Who are you that approaches, sir? ADAPA?
For whom are you wearing the vestments of mourning?"
And ADAPA responded: "In my country two gods have vanished;
Therefore I am dressed in the the vestments of mourning."
And the Gatekeepers asked:
"Who are the two gods who have vanished from your land?"
And ADAPA responded: "DAMMUZ and NINGISHZIDDA, my lords."

The Gatekeepers looked at one another
Bewildered and astonished.
When ADAPA was brought before ANU in the Assembly of the ANUNNAKI.
ANU, King of the Gods, drew ADAPA near to him asking:
"Why have you broken the wings of the South Wind?"
With grace and modesty, ADAPA answered ANU:
"My lord,
I left the House of ENKI to travel by boat across the sea.
I sought to catch fish in the Sea-That-Shines-Like-A-Mirror.
But the South Wind blew and capsized my ship, and so
I was driven to return to the House of ENKI with anger in my heart."
ANU listened patiently.
DAMMUZ and NINGISHZIDDA stirred anxiously.
"But how was it that he was able to command Water and Sky?
How is it that he is able to disturb our workings?
Who is this Man-Child of ENKI?"
They murmured among themselves.
ANU looked upon ADAPA and was silent.
The Assembly of the ANUNNAKI questioned one another:
"Why has ENKI revealed the secrets of Heaven and Earth

To the impure primitive workers?
What new breed of heart ENKI has created within him?
What new breed of mind has ENKI trained?
Has this creature a name? Surely it is not of the ADAMU.
What are we supposed to do with him?"
ANU called for the Food of Life to be brought before him.
ANU called forth for the Waters of Life to be brought before him.
The Food of Life was brought forth. ADAPA did not eat.
The Waters of Life were brought forth. ADAPA did not drink.
ANU looked upon ADAPA and was silent [contemplative].
The vestments were brought forth. ADAPA clothed himself.
The oil was brought forth. ADAPA anointed himself.
ANU looked upon ADAPA and invited:
"Come, now ADAPA, you have not eaten or drunk anything.
We have offered you the Food of Life and the Water of Life
When to others we would offer a banquet of death.
If you do not feast with us you will not gain Eternal Life
And you will not be a god, you will live a short life."

ADAPA bowed to the King of the Gods, ANU.
"I seek not to displease my King,
It is my Lord ENKI who has commanded me not to eat or drink."
ANU smiled commanding that ADAPA be taken back to Earth.
ANU looked upon ADAPA and was contemplatively silent.

OF THE GENERATIONS OF ADAPA ON EARTH[*]

ADAPA and TITI[†] came first.
KAIN and ABAEL were the second generation.
MARDUK instructed ABAEL in shepherding.
NINURTA instructed KAIN in agriculture.
KAIN killed ABAEL and was exiled.[‡]
Other descendants of ADAPA and TITI proliferated in time.
SATI and AZURA were of the third generation.
ENSHI and NOAM were of the fourth generation.
KUNIN and MUALIT were of the fifth generation.
MALULU and DUNNA were of the sixth generation.
IRID and BARAKA were of the seventh generation,

---

[*] Mardukite Catalogue = *Tablet G*
[†] *Titi*—named *"Tiamat"* in some versions.
[‡] In some versions; see *Emesh and Enten* in "*Sumerian Legacy.*"

Who bore ENKIME, mother of SARPANIT.§

SECRETS OF SETH (SATI), SON OF ADAPA*
(WHAT ADAPA LEARNED IN HEAVEN)

The wisest among men and gods have spoken the words:
"In the beginning was the Primordial Chaos and nothing but it existed."
But in truth: the beginning was a Formless Void, the Infinity of Nothingness.
From the center individuated a Divine Spark,‡ the permeating Alpha Spirit.
You are a pure one from a pure power,
You are the first among men,
Because you are the True King on Earth.
Know that I was carried on the summits of Creation,
And made privy to the secrets of the Light, Darkness,
And the habitable worlds in the between.
In the beginning, amidst the Formless Void,
There was Light, Darkness and the Divine Spark between.
In peace and love, the Light was united with the

---

§ *Sarpanit*—wife of the Anunnaki god Marduk and mother of Nabu, as observed in the Mardukite Babylonian Tradition.

* Mardukite Catalogue = *Tablet A*

‡ Equated to "ZU" in the Systemology of Mardukite Zuism.

Word to be one unity.
The Darkness was the [wind] with the Mind in Formless Fire.
In the between was the Divine Spark, the True Light,
Which existed in tranquility [quietness].
Light. Dark. Divine Spark [Spirit]:
These are the Three Roots from the Beginnings.
Each of them existed alone, separated, in their own power,
And in the beginnings, unknown to each other.
The power bestowed upon Light was great.
Light revealed the nature of Darkness and knew its depths.
Light discovered the root of Darkness was not pure [Divine].
In ignorance and isolation, Darkness assumed the Ego-Mind.
Darkness believed none could be above it and it consumed itself.
And Darkness reigned in depths covered by Primordial Waters.
The vileness and corruption beheld by Darkness was not known.
But then Darkness quaked and all could hear the sound.
The Divine Spark heard the sound of the Mind of Darkness,
For the first time did this sound vibrate throughout the Universe.
When Darkness beheld the form of the Divine

Spark [Spirit],
It could not comprehend because the Mind was full of pride.
By the Will of Light: Darkness was separated from the Waters,
Darkness saw its appearance compared to the Divine Spark,
And was overcome with grief.
Darkness sough to assimilate the Divine Spark [Spirit],
Then it sought to make the Divine Spark [Spirit] equal to it.
Both attempts failed. Enraged, the Mind of Darkness was.
It became the Eye of Bitterness in the Depths.
Then it showed its fiery rage at the Heights of the Depths,
In doing so, revealed the nature of the purity of the True Light.
And so failed to Ascend [Come Forth].
Before ADAPA returned to Earth,
The Assembly of the ANUNNAKI stirred
Because ANU was not the sole creator in the Universe.
CHAOS stirred, for the Mind of Darkness was known to be a liar,
When it spoke: "I am God and there is no other."
When after ADAPA had returned to Earth,
The Assembly of ANUNNAKI met with ANU [Chief Creator].
The Assembly asked:

"Isn't this creation [man] who is made in the image
  of a god,
Going to be the ruin of us, and our plans."
The ANUNNAKI and IGIGI murmured among
  themselves.
The god had been made from Earth and Heaven.
It had determined that another was to be made in
  its likeness.
They determined in Heaven:
"Let us also fashion females
By which the man will fall in love with."
And the lesser gods delighted in this decision,
For they feared the rise to power of this new god.
"We are the Powers in this Age.
We are the Rulers in this Age.
Let the Children of Light serve us.
Let the Children of Light be slaves for this entire
  Age."

MARDUK LOSES KINGSHIP IN HEAVEN[*]
(THE FALL OF THE IGIGI)[§]

MARDUK took the Earthling Woman SARPANIT
  as wife.
MARDUK and SARPANIT produced NABU.
ENKI and ENLIL frowned.
"No mere female is SARPANIT," defended
  MARDUK.

---

*   Mardukite Catalogue = *Tablet G*
§   Known in Judeo-Christian sources as the Fall of
    Nephilim or Angels.

"By ADAPA who is Son of ENKI on Earth is
  SARPANIT descended."
Any rights of kingship in Heaven would be
  removed from MARDUK,
To take an Earthing as a spouse, forbidden to the
  gods it was.
To breed with Earthlings, ENKI and ENLIL had
  both become guilty in time,
To take as wives, the IGIGI-WATCHERS sought
  too.
The IGIGI watched the Daughters of Men and saw
  they were beautiful.
Two-hundred of the IGIGI descended.‡
ENLIL spoke with anger:
"Are we to create a new race of gods to rival
  against us?
Bad enough did we bestow upon the primitive
  worker the godly secrets,
Easily did we give away the Heart-of-Heaven-and-
  Earth to ADAPA.
Summon The Lord of the Good Tree,†
Let him accelerate the growth of the Tree of Life
  in man,
Let mankind's years be fixed at one-hundred and
  twenty,
And let none ever partake in the feast of the gods."

---

‡ *"Two-Hundred"*—listed as 100 or 300 in some versions;
  also percentages of "one-third" or "two-thirds" of the
  presumably 300 *"Igigi"* (meaning "watchers" or "the
  seeing ones").

† *Ningishzidda* (presumably).

KINGSHIP ON EARTH (KING-LISTS)*
PRELUDE TO ATRA-ASIS TABLETS

Before the Deluge, kingship was in ERIDU.
ALULIM reigned 8 sars (28,000 years),
Followed by ALAGAR who ruled for 10 sars
  (36,000 years).
Then kingship was moved to BAD-TIBIRA.
EN.ME.EN.LU.AN.NA reigned for 12 sars
  (43,000 years)
Followed by EN.ME.EN.GAL.AN.NA who ruled
  for 8 sars (28,000 years)
And DUMUZI, The Shepherd, for 10 sars (36,000
  years).

INANNA–ISHTAR'S DESCENT
TO THE UNDERWORLD*

This is the chronicle of ISHTAR,
Queen of the Heavens, Mistress of the Gods,
The Brightest Star in the Heavens.
To the nether Land of No Return, to the realm of
  ERESHKIGAL,
ISHTAR, the daughter of NANNA-SIN, she set
  her mind.
From the Great Above she set her mind to the
  Great Below.
The Goddess of the Great Above set her mind

---

* Mardukite Catalogue = *Tablet K*
* Mardukite Catalogue = *Tablet C*

toward the *Great Below*.

To the Darkened Dwelling, the abode of IRKALLA,
To the Black Earth, the lands of CUTHA,
To the house which none may leave, she set her foot,
To the road from which there is no return, she set her foot,
To the cave which accepts no light,
To the place where bowls of dust become food,
To the place where none see light, residing in pure darkness,
To the place where residents are clothed in the wings of birds,
The Lady ISHTAR abandoned Heaven, abandoned Earth,
And to the Underworld she descended.
In ERECH she abandoned EANNA, to the Underworld she descended.
In BADTIBIRA she abandoned EMUSHKALAMMA, to the Underworld she descended.
In ZABALAM she abandoned ESHARRA, to the Underworld she descended.
In ADAB she abandoned ESHARRA, to the Underworld she descended.
In NIPPUR she abandoned BARATUSHGARRA, to the Underworld she descended.
In KISH she abandoned HURSAGKALAMMA, to the Underworld she descended.
In AGADE she abandoned EULMASH, to the

Underworld she descended.
ISHTAR took up the seven Divine Decrees and fixed them to her body,
She sought out the seven Divine Decrees and grasped them in her hand:
The Shugurra, the Starry Crown of ANU she put upon her head,
The Wand of Lapis Lazuli she gripped in her hand,
The Necklace of Lapis Lazuli stones she tied about her neck,
The Brilliant Shinning Stones she took up and carried,
The Golden Ring of Power she placed on her finger,
The Frontlet Amulet she tied as a breastplate,
With the garments of the Queen of Heaven she dressed herself,
And with Holy Oils she anointed herself.
ISHTAR set her mind and moved toward the Underworld,
Her trusted messenger NINSHUBUR walked at her side.
To NINSHUBUR, ISHTAR spoke:
"My trusted friend who are a constant source of support to me,
The messenger of my true words, the carrier of my supporting words,
I tell you that I am descending to the Underworld.
"When I have fully descended to the Underworld,
Fill the spaces of the Heavens with calls of my helplessness,

In the Assembly of ANUNNAKI cry out for my
   blight,
In the House of the Gods create a commotion for
   me,
Lower your eye for me, lower your mouth for me,
Dress for me in the clothing of the poor,
And to the E.KUR, House of ENLIL, fix your
   steps alone for me.
"When you enter the E.KUR, House of ENLIL,
   weep before him:
Father ENLIL, protect your grand-daughter from
   the Gate of Death,
Protect the metal that it may not be ground up to
   dust (in the Underworld).
Protect the stone [lapis lazuli] that it may not be
   broken up (in the Underworld).
Protect the wood [box] from being cut up (in the
   Underworld).
Let not the pure ISHTAR be put to death (in the
   Underworld).
"If ENLIL does not aid you in this matter, then go
   to UR.
When you enter UR, at the E.KISH.SHIRGAL,
House of NANNA, weep before him:
Father NANNA, protect your daughter from the
   Gate of Death,
Protect the metal that it may not be ground up to
   dust (in the Underworld).
Protect the stone [lapis lazuli] that it may not be
   broken up (in the Underworld).
Protect the wood [box] from being cut up (in the

Underworld).
Let not the pure ISHTAR be put to death (in the Underworld).
If NANNA does not aid you in this matter, then go to ERIDU.
"When you enter ERIDU, at the House of ENKI,
Weep before him: Father ENKI, protect your daughter from the Gate of Death,
Protect the metal that it may not be ground up to dust (in the Underworld).
Protect the stone [lapis] that it may not be broken up (in the Underworld).
Protect the wood [box] from being cut up (in the Underworld).
Let not the pure ISHTAR be put to death (in the Underworld).
"Our Father ENKI, the Lord of Wisdom,
Who knows the secret of the food of life, who knows the waters of life,
He will surely listen, he will bring me to life.
Go now, NINSHUBUR, with the word I have commanded thee."
ISHTAR again directed her mind to the Underworld.
To the Lapis Lazuli Castle of ERESHKIGAL in the Underworld she fixed her mind.
To the Gate of the nether Land of No Return, she arrived.
At the Gate to the Underworld, ISHTAR spoke evilly.
In the Castle of the Underworld, ISHTAR acted

evilly.

The Watcher of the Gate, watched.

The Watcher of the Gate, NINGISHZIDDA [Neti], stood fast.

The Serpent of the Deep, NINGISHZIDDA watched ISHTAR approach.

ISHTAR spoke to the Watcher of the Gate:

"Gatekeeper, open your gate to me, Open thy gate so I may enter!

Open, or I will attack the gate! Open, or I will smash the door!

Open, or I will shatter the bars! Open, or I will throw down the walls!

If you will not open wide I will raise the dead!

If you will not open wide I will cause the dead to rise,

So that the dead will outnumber and devour the living!

Spirit of the Watcher of the Gate, open the door!"

The gatekeeper opened his mouth to speak to ISHTAR:

"Stop, my lady, do not throw it down! Who are you?!?"

ISHTAR answered:

"I am the Queen of Heaven, the place where the Sun rises."

"If you are the Queen of Heaven, the place where the Sun rises,

Then why have you come to the Underworld, The Land of No Return?

Why would you take a road where a traveler can

not turn back?
What has caused your heart to lead you here?"
The pure ISHTAR answered him:
"I have come to see my eldest sister ERESHKIGAL,
I have heard her husband GUGALANNA had been killed‡
And I come to witness and respect the funerary rites."
The gatekeeper responded:
"Stay here and keep your place, ISHTAR,
And I will go announce your name to my Queen, ERESHKIGAL."
The gatekeeper entered the castle, saying to ERESHKIGAL:
"My Queen, ERESHKIGAL, your sister ISHTAR is waiting at the gate,
She who comes to uphold the great festivals,
She who stirs up the deep before ENKI [EA], the king.
"In ERECH she abandoned EANNA, to the Underworld she descended.
In BADTIBIRA she abandoned EMUSHKALAMMA, to the Underworld she descended.
In ZABALAM she abandoned ESHARRA, to the Underworld she descended.
In ADAB she abandoned ESHARRA, to the

---

‡ In some versions, *Ishtar's* husband *Dumuzi/Tammuz* is the decesaed.

Underworld she descended.
In NIPPUR she abandoned BARATUSHGARRA,
to the Underworld she descended.
In KISH she abandoned HURSAGKALAMMA,
to the Underworld she descended.
In AGADE she abandoned EULMASH, to the
Underworld she descended.
"ISHTAR took up the seven Divine Decrees and
fixed them to her body,
She sought out the seven Divine Decrees and
grasped them in her hand:
The Shugurra, the Starry Crown of ANU she put
upon her head,
The Wand of Lapis Lazuli she gripped in her hand,
The Necklace of Lapis Lazuli stones she tied about
her neck,
The Brilliant Shinning Stones she took up and
carried,
The Golden Ring of Power she placed on her
finger,
The Frontlet Amulet she tied as a breastplate,
With the garments of the Queen of Heaven she
dressed herself,
And with Holy Oils she anointed herself."
When ERESHKIGAL heard this, she was pale
with fear.
While her lips turned dark she spoke out loud to
herself:
"What moved her heart to me? What compelled
her spirit here?
Should I drink water with the ANUNNAKI?

Should I eat clay for bread and drink dirty water for sustenance?
Should I bemoan the men who have left their wives behind?
Should I bemoan the maidens ripped from the laps of their lovers?
Or should I bemoan the child sent off before his time?"
Then ERESHKIGAL opened her mouth to the gatekeeper:
"Go, gatekeeper, and open the gate for her,
But treat her in accordance with the ancient rules."
The gatekeeper went forth to open the door for her, saying:
"Enter, Lady ISHTAR, the Land of CUTHA will rejoice over thee,
The court of the Land of No Returns will be glad at thy presence."
The Watcher of the Gate loosened the bolts,
And Darkness fell upon the face of ISHTAR.
The Watcher of the Gate opened the door,
And Dark Waters stirred and rose to carry the Goddess of Light.
Of the Gate of GANZIR, the Watcher opened.
NINGISHZIDDA opened the Gate to the Land of No Return.
And ISHTAR entered.
When at the First Gate ISHTAR entered,
NINSIGHZIDDA removed the Starry Crown of Heaven (from her head).
And ISHTAR asked: "Why, Serpent, have you

taken the First Jewel?"
And the Serpent answered:
"This is the Covenant of Old, the Rules of the
  Mistress of the Underworld,
Enter, my lady, the First Gate."
When at the Second Gate ISHTAR entered,
NINSIGHZIDDA removed the Wand of Lapis
  Lazuli (from her hands).
And ISHTAR asked: "Why, NETI, have you taken
  the Second Jewel?"
And NETI answered:
"This is the Covenant of Old, the Rules of the
  Mistress of the Underworld,
Enter, my lady, the Second Gate."
When at the Third Gate ISHTAR entered,
NINSIGHZIDDA removed the Lapis Lazuli
  Necklace (from her neck).
And ISHTAR asked: "Why, Gatekeeper, have you
  taken the Third Jewel?"
And the Gatekeeper answered:
"This is the Covenant of Old, the Rules of the
  Mistress of the Underworld,
Enter, my lady, the Third Gate."
When at the Fourth Gate ISHTAR entered,
NINSIGHZIDDA removed the Shinning Brilliant
  Stones (from her waistband?).
And ISHTAR asked: "Why, Guardian of the Gate,
  have you taken the Fourth Jewel?"
And the Guardian of the Gate answered:
"This is the Covenant of Old, the Rules of the
  Mistress of the Underworld,

Enter, my lady, the Fourth Gate."
When at the Fifth Gate ISHTAR entered,
NINSIGHZIDDA removed the Golden Ring of
 Power (from her finger).
And ISHTAR asked: "Why, Watcher of the Portal,
 have you taken the Fifth Jewel?"
And the Watcher of the Portal answered:
"This is the Covenant of Old, the Rules of the
 Mistress of the Underworld,
Enter, my lady, the Fifth Gate."
When at the Sixth Gate ISHTAR entered,
NINSIGHZIDDA removed the Breastplate of
 Righteousness.
And ISHTAR asked: "Why, NINNKIGAL, have
 you taken the Sixth Jewel?"
And NINNKIGAL answered:
"This is the Covenant of Old, the Rules of the
 Mistress of the Underworld,
Enter, my lady, the Sixth Gate."
When at the Seventh Gate ISHTAR entered,
NINSIGHZIDDA stripped the Vestments of
 Queenship (from her body).
And ISHTAR asked: "Why, Ancient Messenger,
 have you taken the Seventh Jewel?"
And the Ancient Messenger answered:
"This is the Covenant of Old, the Rules of the
 Mistress of the Underworld,
Enter, my lady, the Seventh Gate."
ISHTAR had descended to the Underworld.
To the depths of CUTHA, land of KUR did
 ISHTAR descend.

Lost were the Seven Decrees[‡] of the Upper World.
Lost were the Seven Powers of the Land of the Living.
Lost was the sustenance of the Food of Life and Waters of Life.
ISHTAR then appeared before ERESHKIGAL.
ERESHKIGAL saw her presence and screamed.
ISHTAR advanced toward ERESHKIGAL.
ERESHKIGAL summoned NAMMTAR, the Black Magician,
Saying these words as she spoke to him:
"Go, NAMMTAR, imprison her in Darkness in my castle!
Release against her the Seven ANUNNAKI
Release against her the Sixty Demons of the Deep:
Demons of the eyes against her eyes! Demons of the sides against her sides!
Demons of the heart against her heart! Demons of the feet against her feet!
Demons of the head against her head! Against her whole body, Demons of KUR!"
The ANUNNAKI, the Seven Judges of Death, fixed eyes of Death upon her,
At their word, the word which conjures all Demons,
The Demons came to tear apart ISHTAR from all sides.
In the Land of KUR, ISHTAR was killed.

[‡] Interpreted as Divine *Me*, "discs of power," "jewels" or "talismans." Refer also to "*The Tablets of Destiny*" by Joshua Free and its foreword by Reed Penn.

The body of ISHTAR was shredded into a corpse.
And the corpse was suspended on a cross [stake].
For three days and three nights ISHTAR hung.
When after the three days and nights had passed,
The messenger of ISHTAR, NINSHUBAR,
The messenger of the favorable words of ISHTAR,
The carrier of the supporting words of ISHTAR,
NINSHUBAR filled the Heavens with laments for ISHTAR,
NINSHUBAR cried for her in the Assembly of the Gods,
NINSHUBAR caused commotion in the House of the Lord,
He lowered his eye for her, he lowered his mouth for her,
Like a poor servant he appealed to the Gods for her.
To the E.KUR, house of ENLIL, alone he directed his travels.
But Father ENLIL did not stand by him in this matter.
To the EKISHSHIRGAL, House of NANNA, he directed his steps.
But Father NANNA did not stand by him in this matter.
To ERIDU, in the house of ENKI, he wearily moved.
Our Father ENKI, listened to the words of NINSHUBAR.
ENKI listened to the words of the descent of ISHTAR.

ENKI listened to the words of lament for ISHTAR.
ENKI listened to the words describing the opening of GANZIR.
Father ENKI answered NINSHUBAR:
"What has my daughter done now? I am troubled. What has ISHTAR done?
I am troubled. What has the Queen of the Heavens done? I am troubled.
What has she done!"
Father ENKI summoned forth clay to fashion a KURGARRU.
Father ENKI summoned forth wind to fashion a KALATURRU.
From the clay and the wind ENKI summoned two elementals.
ENKI fashioned the KURGARRU, Spirit of the Earth.
ENKI fashioned the KALATURRU, Spirit of the Deep.
ENKI, to the KURGARRU, gave the Food of Life.
ENKI, to the KALATURRU, gave the Water of Life.
To the Elementals ENKI spoke:
"Arise and set your mind to travel to the GANZIR Gate,
To the Gate of the Underworld, set your feet,
To the nether Land of No Return, fix your eyes.
The Seven Gates of the Underworld will open to you
And no charm or spell can keep you away, for upon you I have set my Number.

Take up the Food of Life and the Water of Life,
And ERESHKIGAL shall not harm you.
ERESHKIGAL shall not raise her arm against you.
ERESHKIGAL shall have no power over you.
Upon the corpse of ISHTAR hung from the cross [stake],
Direct the Fear of the Rays of the Secret Fire,
Sixty times sprinkle the Food of Life,
Sixty times sprinkle the Waters of Life,
Sprinkle sixty times upon the corpse, and surely ISHTAR will rise."
Like winged serpents the elementals flew.
To the GANZIR Gate the elementals flew invisibly.
Invisible, they passed by the Gatekeeper unseen.
Through the Seven Gates the elementals flew invisibly.
Invisible, they passed by the Seven Watchers unseen.
With haste they entered into the Castle of Darkness,
In the Castle of Death they beheld horrible sights,
But with haste they moved, stopping only at the corpse of ISHTAR.
ISHTAR, the Beautiful Queen of Heaven.
ISHTAR, the Mistress of the Gods of Heaven.
ISHTAR, the Lady of Priestesses of UR.
ISHTAR, the Brightest Star of the Heavens.
ISHTAR, the Beloved of ENKI, she hung from the cross [stake] bleeding,
From one thousand critical wounds ISHTAR hung

bleeding.
KURGARRU and KALATURRA approached the body of ISHTAR.
ERESHKIGAL, sensing their presence, screamed.
KURGARRU directed the Rays of Fire upon the Queen of Death.
KALATURRA directed Rays of Fire upon the Queen of Death.
ERESHKIGAL, while powerful in CUTHA, retreated.
KURGARRU, upon the corpse of ISHTAR,
Sprinkled the Food of Life of ENKI sixty times.
KALATURRA, upon the corpse of ISHTAR,
Sprinkled the Water of Life of ENKI sixty times.
Upon the corpse of ISHTAR, Queen of the Heavens,
KURGARRU and KALATURRA directed the Spirit of Life of ENKI.
ISHTAR rose!
ISHTAR ascended from the Underworld!
The ANUNNAKI fled their thrones of gold,
And the spirits of the nether Land of No Returns,
The spirits who had descended to the Dead peacefully,
When ISHTAR ascended from the Underworld,
When ISHTAR ascended on the winged serpents of ENKI,
ISHTAR ascended through the Gates of GANZIR and NETI,
Surely the dead hastened ahead of her.
When ISHTAR ascended past the First Gate,

The Queen of Heaven took back her jeweled
Robes of Royalty.
When ISHTAR ascended past the Second Gate,
The Queen of Heaven took back her jeweled
Breastplate of Righteousness.
When ISHTAR ascended past the Third Gate,
The Queen of Heaven took back her jeweled Ring
of Gold.
When ISHTAR ascended past the Fourth Gate,
The Queen of Heaven took back her jeweled
Shinning Stones.
When ISHTAR ascended past the Fifth Gate,
The Queen of Heaven took back her jeweled
Necklace.
When ISHTAR ascended past the Sixth Gate,
Queen of Heaven took back her jeweled Wand of
Lapis Lazuli.
When ISHTAR ascended past the Seventh Gate,
Queen of Heaven took back her jeweled Starry
Crown of ANU.
And the spirits of the Dead rose,
And the spirits of the Dead preceded ISHTAR
through the Gates.
And ERESHKIGAL was scorned.
The Scorned Queen ERESHKIGAL spoke a
powerful curse.
Against the Queen of Heavens ERESHKIGAL
spoke her curse.
And NAMMTAR manifested the curse.
When DUMUZI [*Tammuz*], the Lover of ISHTAR
Goes down before me through the GANZIR Gate

of Death,
When the lamentations of the people come with him,
When DUMUZI, the Lover of ISHTAR is dead and buried,
May the Dead rise and smell the incense!

PRELUDE TO ATRA-ASIS (KING-LISTS)[*]

Then kingship was moved to LARAK and EN.SIB.ZI.AN.NA ruled for 8 sars (28,800 years),
And kingship was moved to SHIPPAR [ZIMBIR] where EN.ME.EN.DUR.AN.NA ruled for 5 sars and 5 ners (21,000 years).
Then kinship was moved to SHURUPPAK [SHURUPPAG] where UBARA.TUTU was ruling for 5 sars and 5 ners (18,600 years),
And then the Great Deluge swept over the Earth.

THE DISPOSAL OF HUMANITY (ATRA-ASIS)[*]

The population of mankind increased in generations,
Until such time their calamities were disturbing the ANUNNAKI.
The gods of the day learned of a horrific natural disaster pending,

---

[*] Mardukite Catalogue = *Tablet K*
[*] Mardukite Catalogue = *Tablet G*

The Destroyer had arrived and the disturbance on Earth would be great.
IGIGI and ANUNNAKI allowed mankind to perish unwarned.
ENKI had given his blood to a line of men and found he could not be so harsh.
MARDUK had given his blood to a line of men and could not be harsh.
To the final descendants in their line, they sent a dream.
To the mind of ATRA-ASIS, ENKI filled with a warning dream.
To the mind of ATRA-ASIS, MARDUK filled with special instructions.
To ATRA-HASIS they revealed that ENLIL acted with hate.
ENLIL, Father of the People, wished them dead.
ATRA-ASIS received the dream and prayed to ENKI:
"Lord, give me discernment to understand the meaning of the dream.
Give me the knowing so that I may be prepared for the consequences."
ENKI answered the young servant:
"While you kneel in your bedroom, listen out your window to the words.
Pay attention, because I cannot speak with you. Do you understand?
I am talking to the reed bush outside your window,
I am talking to the walls of your shelter,
But I cannot speak with you lest I invite the wrath

to my doorstep.
By the Covenant of the ANUNNAKI, I have said nothing to you this day."

And ENKI spoke:

"Wall: listen to me. Reed bush: pay attention.

Leave your house in your father's land immediately and build a boat.

Give up all of your material possessions in order to save your life.

Such a boat has never been constructed on Earth and it must be strong.

The roof must be like the hull if it is to survive a journey to the *Great Beneath*,

So that the sun shall not see any of the parts within.

The boat you build will be two-hundred feet tall,

And the height should be divided in seven so that it has six decks.

When the people ask you why you are constructing such a thing:

Tell them that the God of Man, ENLIL, hates you all,

ENLIL has deemed you unfit to any longer reside in the cities,

Or to walk the surface of the Earth, which is commanded by ENLIL,

So you must now seek refuge in the *Great Beneath*,

To survive, you will go to the domain of your Lord ENKI,

And I, ENKI, will shower abundances down upon

you later."
ENKI opened the "water clock" [time-piece] and filled it.
ENKI set the "water clock" on the window sill saying:
"Remember, I have not said these words to you.
In seven days, your time will be up.
The Deluge will be upon you. Go! Make haste!"
ATRA-ASIS received the command from ENKI,
And he drew together an Assembly of Elders at his Gate.
ATRA-ASIS spoke to the Elders:
"My fellow man, my god does not agree with your god,
As ENKI and ENLIL are constantly in discord with each other.
They have expelled me from this land for my alignment to ENKI.
I can not live in the city any longer among you.
Nor will I be allowed to set my feet on the Earth of ENLIL.
I will go to dwell with my god ENKI in the *Great Beneath*.
My Lord ENKI has commanded me to come to his abode in a boat."
The boat was constructed and then a feast was enjoyed and all were invited.
Seven days passed for the family of ATRA-ASIS.
MARDUK installed the Tablets; the Tablets had been brought on board.
ENKI installed the memory; the memory had been

brought on board.
The "Cattle-God" had brought the creatures on board.
ATRA-ASIS had brought his family on board.
Much celebration was there in the hearts of his family,
No peace and no rest was there for ATRA-ASIS.
While the others ate and played, he went on top of the ship to wait.
Very soon thereafter, the appearance of the weather began to change.
ADAD, The "Storm-God" grew restless in the clouds.
Immediately, he called to bring tar and pitch to seal the door,
The securing rope had been cut to release the boat,
And by the time the door had been bolted,
The wind-storm had been raised in the sky.
The Deluge raged forth, like the stamping Bull of Heaven.

THE NEW TESTAMENT OF

PRIESTS

AND KINGS ON THIS EARTH

A collection of the most ancient Mardukite cuneiform records accounting for activities of the Mesopotamian Anunnaki pantheon and their Priests, Priestesses and Dragon-Kings
—*specifically those overseeing the systems of Planet Earth and the Human Condition.*

ATRA-ASIS ADDENDUM (KING-LISTS)*

The Deluge ended the Kingship of the
   ANUNNAKI "Gods" on Earth.
After the Deluge, the decree of Kingship again
   came down from Heaven,
And the rule of the demigods began with
GA-UR [NGUSHUR] for 1,200 years,
GULLA-NIDABA [KULLASSINA-BEL] for
   960 years,
NANGISHLISHMA for 670 years and
   ENTARAHANA for 420 years,
BABUUM for 360 years and PUANNUM for
   840 years,
GALIBUUM [KALIBUM] for 960 years,
KALUMUMU [KALUMUM] for 840 years,
KAGAGIIB [ZUKAKIP] for 900 years and ABA
   [ATAB] for 600 years,
ATABBA [MASHDA] Son of ATAB for
   840 years,
ARPIUM [ARWIUM] Son of MASHDA for
   720 years.
ETANA, The Shepherd, ascended to the Heavens,
And returned to Earth to begin his dynasty.
Again, Kingship had been lowered from the
   Heavens and
ETANA ruled for 1,500 years when Kingship was
   moved to URUK,
And so ended the rule of the demigods and began
   the rule of the earthborn deities.

---

* Mardukite Catalogue = *Tablet K*

THE WORLD ORDER OF ENKI*

Lord ENKI who most nobly travels the Heavens and Earth,
Father ENKI, self-reliant, offspring of the Bull of Heaven,
Prized by ENLIL, KUR, and loved by the holy ANU of Heaven,
Lord ENKI planted the Tree of ABZU in in ERIDU,
Its shade spreading over the Heavens—its grove spreading across the Earth.
ENKI, Lord of the ANUNNAKI, Strong One of ANU and URAS,
NUDIMMUD, the Mighty One of the E.KUR.
ENKI lifts his eye and observes where the bison is born,
And where the stag is born, and where the sheep is born,
In the meadows, in the place where no one dares enter, he fixes his eye.
At the command of ENKI the grain is heaped and piled up.
At the command of ENKI the harvest of the land is fruitful.
At the command of ENKI the sheep in the field are plentiful.
At the command of ENKI the shepherd is called forth to work the field.

---

* Mardukite Catalogue = *Tablet K*

At the command of ENKI the woman is called
   forth to churn next to him.
The meals are set forth by clean workers in the
   dining halls of the Gods.
The lords and rulers are thrilled and come to feast
   in joy.
ENKI, Lord of Wisdom, Beloved of ANU,
   Supreme Name in ERIDU,
ENKI, who directs the commands and decisions of
   ANUNNAKI on Earth,
Except on the day of the fate declared for mankind
   in the Deluge.
You have locked up the Gate by day and have
   brought down the Stars.
You have calculated the Unknowable Number in
   the Universe,
And have fashioned the wheel in which months
   enter the mansions.
You have allowed mankind to live and given them
   a place to call home.
ENKI, you have commanded the watch over your
   creation.
Father ENKI, walk among the fertile land, may it
   bear healthy seed.
NUDUMMID, walk among the cattle, may they
   give healthy birth.
ENKI, Lord of ABZU, when you walk among
   stacked grains in the field,
Celebrate in your offering as is your holy right,
My Father, who is the ruler of above and below.
And ENKI said: "I am the true offspring

Who was sprung from the wild Bull of Heaven.
I am a leading son of ANU who storms over the Great Below.
I am the great lord who rules over all the lands.
I am the first ruler among the rulers and the maker of kings on Earth.
I am the father of all the lands and eldest brother of the ANUNNAKI Gods,
Who seals the Gates both above and below.
I am cunning and wise in the lands who directs justice alongside ANU.
I am the one NINTU truly loves and who NINHURSAG gave a good name.
I am the leading son of ANU, Lord of all the ANUNNAKI."
At the command of ENKI the stalls for sheep were built.
The fields were sown and ENKI poured water from the HEGAL upon them.
At the place where the stalks were piled up a shrine was built,
A good name it was given: the "Pure Place."
A shrine was built to decree good fates in the ABZU.
The sacred spells and litanies were recorded on tablets in the ABZU.
The lands of MAGAN and TILMUN [Dilmun] set eyes upon ENKI.
The gold and silver was transported to NIPPUR for inspection by ENLIL.
The great eye of ENKI sweeps the land, watching

over and protecting,
The great eye of ENKI is foremost everywhere, above and below.
Praise to you ENKI, Lord of above and below,
Who all the priests of ERIDU and SUMER praise,
As is seen in the religious rites in the ABZU.
Great Gods of the ANUNNAKI, stand watch over the holy places,
Cleanse the House with your presence and purify the shrines.
The ANUNNAKI have taken up their dwellings in your midst,
And they consume the food harvested by the workers in the fields.
In the Great House in SUMER, many stalls were built,
And cows did multiply, and the shrines were built up to the Heavens.
ENKI, Lord of the ABZU, decreed the fate for the Shrine of UR.
ENKI crossed to the TILMUN [Dilmun], cleansing and purifying it.
Lagoons were placed near the beautiful shrine full of fish.
Palm trees were planted in its fertile fields dull of dates.
But devouring power, ENLIL attacked the walls, stealing the Gold, silver and lapis, and returning it to NIPPUR.
The attack of ENLIL occurred when ENKI had turned his eye from there,

And had instead returned to the EUPHRATES
(river) and stood like a bull,
There he filled the waters with his own life and
also the TIGRIS (river).
The water he brought was flowing with life and
sweet as wine.
The waters fed life to fields and the grain was
raised to be eaten.
Another holy shrine was raised, its interior like
a maze,
With a lower station built to follow the IKU-
constellation,
And with an upper station built to follow the
Chariot.‡
And the ANUNNAKI Gods dared not go near this
place,
Except when humbled in prayer and supplication.
To establish kingship, ENKI dripped the
dragonblood on the shrines,
The lines of kingship on the Earth were so
designated from Heaven,
And he gave to the king a the starry crown to wear,
And to the king he gave the lapis lazuli
implements,
Fastening to his line the lapis lazuli diadem.†
The good earth was lavished with flourishing
vegetation.
ENKI multiplied the herds in the fields and

---

‡ A constellation (presumably).
† *"Diadem"*—a jeweled crown, headband, or recognized symbol of absolute authority.

pastures,
And set them in their place allowing them to breed together.
The lofty and powerful hand of ENLIL was passed on,
To SUMUGAN, the King in the HURSAG, it was placed in charge.
The kings were decided and the borders of the realms were decided.
The ANUNNAKI were called forth and given their charged.
Great cities were raised and filled by the Queens of the birth-giving.
To these ANUNNAKI Queens, the birth of kings they were charged.
And so by the decree of ENKI did the dragon blood rule over the Earth.

PRELUDE TO AKKADIAN SUMER (KING-LISTS)*

BALIIH, son of ETANA, ruled for 400 years and
ENMENUNNA for 660 and MELAMKISH for 900 and
BARRAKNUNNA for 1,200 and MESZA for 140 and TIIZKAR for 300
And ILKUU for 1,200 and IITASADUUM for 1,200 years
And ENMEENBARAGISI for 900.

---

* Mardukite Catalogue = *Tablet K*

The Dynasty of URUK is marked
With the rule of AGGA for 625 years, followed by his son MESHKIAGGASHER,
Descended of UTU but after 325 years of rule,
He entered the Great Deep and disappeared.
The son of MESHKIAGGASHER built up URUK strongly,
His name is ENMERKAR and he ruled for 420 years.
LUGALBANDA ruled 1,200 years and DUMUZI for 100.
The last of the famous Earthborn deities is GILGAMESH,‡
Who was fathered by a spirit and ruled for 126 years.
Then UR-NUNGAL took up the rule for 130 years,
Which ended the age of "long life ruling" in URUK as UTUL-KALAMA [UDUL-KALAMMA] ruled only 15 years
And LABASHER [LABASHUM] ruled only 9 years and
ENNUNADANNA [ENNUNTARAHANA] ruled only 8 years and MESHHE [MESH-HEHE] "the blacksmith" ruled only 36 years
And MELEMANA [MLAMANNA] rules only 6 years,
The first dynasty ending with the 36 year rule of

---

‡ The Sumerian *Epic of Gilgamesh* does not appear in Mardukite Babylonian versions of the Anunnaki Bible.

LUGALKIAGA [LUGAIKITUM].

In UR, the first dynasty descended from
MESHANEPADA [80 yr],
MESHKIAGGA-NANNA [36 yr],
ELULU [25 yr] and BALULU [36 yr].

In AWAN, there Three Kings ruled [names unknown].

When Kingship passed to the dynasty of KISH‡

The bloodline was carried by SUSUDA [200 yr] and DADASIG [81 yr], MAMAGAL [360 yr], KALBUM [195 yr], TUGE [360 yr], MEN-NUNNA [180 yr], EN[B]I-ISHTAR [290 yr] and LUGALN[G]U [360 yr]

Before the Kingship was observed in LAGASH:
UR-NANSHE [30 yr], AKURGAL [9 yr], ENNATUM [30 yr], ENANNATUM I [20 yr], ENTEMENA [22 yr], ENANNATUM II [9 yr], ENENTARZI [5 yr], LUGALANDA [5 yr] and URUINIMGINA [9 yr].

For a short time the Dynasty of HAMAZI rules
And was carried out by HADANISH for 360 years.

And then Kingship was returned to URUK [UNUG]

Which was begun with ENSHAGKUSHANNA [60 yr]

And LUGALKINSHEDUDU [LUGALURE] [120 yrs]

---

‡ Presumably c. 26th Century B.C.

(a contemporary of ENTEMENA who ruled in LAGASH),
Followed by ARGANDEA [7 yr] before being defeated,
And then Kingship was returned to UR [URIM],
With a dynasty from NANNA [120 yr]
Followed by his son MESHKIAN[G]NANNA [48 yr], then LUGALANEMUNDU [90 yr] carried the line to ADAB.
And then ANBU put forth the Dynasty of MARI.†
The line continued with ANBA [17 yr], BAZI [30 yr], ZIZI [20 yr], LIMER "the GUDUG priest" [30 yr]
And finally SHARRUMITER [9 yr]
Before the MARI Dynasty was defeated
And Kingship resumed in KISH.
KUG-BAU [KUBABA] ruled in KISH for 100 years
Before Kingship in KISH was rivaled with the AKSHAK Dynasty
Though remained in KISH after the rule of UNZI [30 yr], UN[D]-ALULU [6 yr], UR-UR [6 yr], PUZURNIRAH [20 yr], ISHUIL [24 yr] and SHU-SUEN(SIN) [7 yr].
The line of KUG-BAU [KUBABA] continued in KISH by PUZU[R]-SUEN(SIN) [25 yr], UR-ZABABA [6 yr/400 yr?], ZIMUDAR [30 yr], USI-WATAR [7 yr], ESHTARMUTI [11 yr], ISHMESHAMMASH [11 yr], SHU-ILISHU [15

---

† Presumably c. 25th Century B.C.

yr] and NANNIYA [7 yr],
And then LUGALZA[GG]ESI ruled in URUK for 25 years.
In ancient AKKAD, SARGON was cup-bearer to UR-ZABABA in KISH
Before becoming the King of the Realm of AGADE‡ [40 yr]
And defeating LUGALZA[GG]ESI in URUK, thereby ruling SUMER,
Followed with the descent of RIMUSH [9 yr], MANISHTISHU [15 yr], NARAM-SUEN(SIN) [56 yr]
And SHARKALISH [SHARGANI] [25 yr].
Then in three years time, IRGIGI, IMI, NANUM and ILULU ruled.
Afterward, reign was with DU-DU [21 yr], SHUDUR-UL(KIB) [15 yr]

ENLILSHIP OF MARDUK ON EARTH[*]

The Bull of Heaven, The Lord of the Deep.
ENKI, son of ANU, brought forth MARDUK.
MARDUK, Lord of the Pure Mound was created.
MARDUK, Created to be worthy of prayer.
MARDUK, Created to be worthy of sacrifice.
The evil-doer who would bring falsehood before MARDUK,
He brings death upon his whole country.

---

‡ *Agade*—alternative name for *Akkad*.
* Mardukite Catalogue = *Tablet L*

Let you never break your contract, whether with the righteous or the evil-doer.

Both the faithful and unfaithful walk Beneath the ever-present Eye of MARDUK.

Water brings life to the one who drinks the Truth.

Fire brings clarity to the path of one who walks with Truth.

Air brings inspiration to the one who breathes the Truth.

Earth brings foundation to the one who stands on Truth,

The Tablets of the Law have been written and sealed,

At the Foundation [Bond] of Heaven and Earth.

Offer daily the sacrifice of meat and libation to MARDUK,

And let the Altar of Offering never be emptied.

May MARDUK bring his brightness and glory to the people.

May MARDUK bring help to the troubles of the people.

May MARDUK bring ease to the suffering of the people.

May MARDUK bring joy to the sadness of the people.

May MARDUK bring mercy to the unjustness of the people.

May MARDUK bring health to the illness of the people.

May MARDUK bring victory the the warriors in his name.

May MARDUK bring good conscience to priests of his name.
May MARDUK bring a happy and prosperous home to the people of his nation who live under the Law of MARDUK,
Who was given Enlilship on Earth as appropriated by ANU, the Heavenly Bull, who lives and resides in Heaven.

THE SARGON TABLET[*]

I am SARGON, the Mighty King of AKKAD.
My mother was of humble estate; I knew nothing of my father.
The brother of my father was a Dweller in the Mountain.
My city is AZUR-PIRANI (Which lies on the banks of the Euphrates River)
My humble mother brought me forth in secret.
In a basket of reeds she laid me, she smeared the latch with bitumen
And pushed me off into the river.
But the river did not swallow me.
The river carried me to AKKI (A man who labored by watering the fields)
AKKI lifted me out of the basket, raised me as his son.
AKKI reared me to be his gardener,
And all the while I gardened, MARDUK smiled

---

[*] Mardukite Catalogue = *Tablet L*

on me.
And by this love, I was made a Ruler of the Kingdom.

A LAMENT FOR BABYLON AND THE LAST DAYS OF EARTH[*]

Holy vision. Holy vision. What do I behold before me?
The skies are filled with terror.
The earth quakes beneath my feet.
When out my window I expected daylight, only darkness has come.
In the skies the clouds of doom gathered and rained forth death.
When the glow of lightning ceased, all was again washed in darkness,
And everything that had lived, had turned to ash.
During the age of ISHTAR,
During the rule of AKKAD, SHARU-KIN (SARGON),
MARDUK turned his head,
Poor BABYLON had done sacrilege.
Everywhere from east to west the day had to turned into darkness.
The current of the river had changed its course and flow,
And the eyes of the god had looked away,
The land was to perish,

---

[*] Mardukite Catalogue = *Tablet R*

And the eyes of the god had looked away,
The people were to perish.
But this is nothing compared to what will come in the Last Days.
That which will be done was never done before on Earth.
In the Last Days, the Earth will completely perish of human life,
And the land will be damaged so as not to support life,
And the skies will be darkened so as not to allow the light of Sun,
And nothing will be allowed to live on Earth.
First the evil blast and then the baneful storm,
The heavens will be severed in two and the Earth will be impaled.
The face of the Earth will be smite as never before.
In the days of the Destroyer this nearly happened;
When the Earth darkened, the shadow was passed over the face
And the Evil Wind was born anew.
You were given Kingship on Earth
But an eternal reign you were not granted.
Again MARDUK comes to build the Foundation of Heaven-Earth,‡

---

‡ *Heaven-Earth*—in Sumerian, "*An-Ki*" usually denoting all of creation ("Heaven" and "Earth"); appearing in references to early Anunnaki ziggurat-temple headquarters, such as *Dur-An-Ki*, the "*Foundation of Heaven-Earth*" or *E.Temen.An.Ki*, the "*Temple of*

And the unknown sovereign [of the faith] will come to his aid,
And he will be known hence as the "Triumphant Son-Man."
The armies of MARDUK will conquer the unjust
And the wrong-doer, the [aligned] people living in his time
Will rejoice in their freedom, but woe to the unprepared
Who have not learned the secrets of the ages.
Then will a new king rise in BABYLON,
Beside the prophet he sits.
A new temple to the Heavens will be raised;
A new BABYLON will rise.
The Foundation of Heaven-Earth will stand like a mountainside.[†]
And the "Gateway of the Gods"[∞] will be opened!
There the servants of MARDUK will grasp his hand,
To lead the Risen God in procession to the triumphant throne.

   Heaven-Earth."
[†] The stepped-pyramid construction style of ziggurat temples (and presumably other pyramids) were intended to represent the mountains; although we know that the geometry (shape) also has other energetic properties.
[∞] *Gateway of the Gods*—in Akkadian, *Bab-Ilu*, alternatively the "*Gate of AN*" or "*Stairway to Heaven*," "*Ladder of Lights*," &tc.

MARDUKITE KINGSHIP IS AUTHORIZED IN BABYLON (KING-LISTS)[*]

In ancient BABYLON, SU[MU]-ABU [24 yr] was given Kingship,
Followed by SUMU-LA-ILU(EL) [36 yr] ZABU [SABUM] [15 yr], ABIL-SIN [APIL-SUEN] [18 yr], SIN-MUBALIT [20 yr]
And then HAMMURABI[‡]
Who received the Book of the Law from MARDUK.

THE LAW OF MARDUK TABLET[*]

ANU, Supreme King of the ANUNNAKI and ENLIL, Lord of Heaven on Earth,
Assigned the fate of the land to MARDUK,
The ruling heir of EA [ENKI], God of Righteousness.
Dominion was granted to MARDUK in BABYLON over mankind,
Great among the IGIGI [Watchers] was he, and great was his name.
On the name of MARDUK was built the everlasting kingdom of Heaven on Earth,
And on the Foundation of Heaven and Earth was kingship decided.
Among the kings of BABYLON, MARDUK

---

[*] Mardukite Catalogue = *Tablet K*
[‡] Translated as *Khammurabi* in some versions.
[*] Mardukite Catalogue = *Tablet L*

descended on the Exalted Prince,
HAMMURABI, a servant of the Lord MARDUK,
Called to bring order in the lands of MARDUK
By the law that would destroy the wicked
   sorcerers and evil-doers in the land,
And that the strong would not rise up and
   overcome the weak and install another slavery,
The ADAMU would not be slaved again to toil for
   the IGIGI,
Or to be a slave again among their own race.
The Eye of MARDUK passed onto and rested
   upon HAMMURABI,
To whom was given the Dragonblood of BEL‡
   made prosperous,
Who reestablished ERIDU and purified the
   worship at the shrines,
True patron to the E.KUR and rejoicer in the name
   of MARDUK,
To whom he makes daily prayer and offering as he
   was directed.
He is beloved by the god NABU and ADAD
   listens to his prayers.
"Hear me," said the King, "who holds the Naval of
   the Four Corners,
I have come, led to this place by the rays which
   shine over the land,

---

‡   "*Bel*"—a general Semitic term for "Lord." Applied
    exclusively to *Enlil* on most older Sumerian tablet
    sources; occasionally to *Enki*, but more often *Marduk*,
    in more recent Akkadian and Chaldeo-Babylonian
    sources.

Beloved of MARDUK, I have been sent forth by
   the kings above,
By the name of MARDUK, I have been given rule
   over mankind.
In the name of MARDUK protection granted
   throughout the land.
By the powers of MARDUK is righteousness
   commanded on Earth.
In the grace of MARDUK the oppressed on Earth
   shall live as
Free men as lavishly as the great god SAMAS has
   enjoyed life."
Then was HAMMURABI shown the Secret
   Tablets of Destiny,
And from it he set down the Book of the Law to
   preserve justice,
The code was to be given to the Dragonblood of
   the generations,
That justice would prevail throughout the Earth
   forever after.
To live in harmony with one another was the
   decree,
That no man should take up arms against another,
   or steal from another.
That any man who borrows from another shall
   make good for it,
And under the blessings of MARDUK, none
   should ever be in want.
A righteous law was established in the land as was
   taught from Heaven.
HAMMURABI went out to teach the Law of

MARDUK to the people,
Protector of the People, he did not withdraw into secret cavities.
He was not negligent with the people given to him by BEL.
He was not negligent with the laws given to him by SAMAS.
He was not negligent with the power to rule given to him by MARDUK.
Overcoming all else, the King allowed the Light to shine upon the land.
"Hear me," said the King. "The ANUNNAKI gods have called to me.
NERGAL and ISHTAR have entrusted to me Terrible Weapons,
EA [ENKI] has entrusted me with the clear sight to rule the lands of men,
MARDUK has entrusted me wisdom to subdue all enemies,
And I go forth to subdue the Earth and let prosperity reign in all the lands.
Security to live should be the guarantee of all men in their homes,
Disturbing the peace and order in the land cannot be tolerated."
The King continued: "I am the straight-staff bearing shepherd.
I am a lover of the people of the lands of SUMER and AKKAD,
And under my rule [shelter], may all the people find sanctuary,

That the strong-armed will not injure the weaker,
And too shall widows and orphans be protected in my city of BABYLON,
Where ANU, BEL, EA [ENKI] and MARDUK smile upon us,
In the E.SAGILU Temple of MARDUK, which stands on the Foundation of Heaven-Earth,
Where all injuries are healed and all disputes are settled."
HAMMURABI is a ruler [king], but more so, he is a father to the people,
And he holds the words and law of MARDUK in high reverence,
Who has achieved victory in the name of MARDUK, Above and Below,
Bestower of the beneficent grace of the ANUNNAKI on his subjects,
He who has established the Order of MARDUK in the lands.
Among rulers his words will be well considered, no wisdom is equal.
By the command of SAMAS,[†] the Judge of the Heaven and Earth,
May truth and righteousness reign supreme throughout the lands.
Let those who read these words have a pure heart and pray
To MARDUK, my Lord and SARPANIT, my Lady, his consort.

[†] *Samas*—transcribed as *Šamaš* or "*Shammash*."

May the Elder Gods of the ANUNNAKI who visit the shrine of BABYLON,
Grant to the pure their desires, such as those taken to MARDUK daily.
By the Order of MARDUK, may no destruction see the great temple.
To the future generations, may they heed all of these words set down,
Let the law of the land not be altered from that which I have given it.
A wise ruler is one who is sure to understand these words.

"By the decree of SAMAS, I have been given my Eternal Legacy,
My words [legacy] shall always be in the mouths of the people on Earth,
That my name shall be ever visible in the Great Book,
And the wisdom of the Great Book shall ever be in the hands of Dragonblood.
If a forthcoming ruler should read my words and not corrupt the law,
Then may SAMAS extend the length of his reign on Earth,
And he shall ever reign in righteousness over his subjects."

NERGAL ATTACKS BABYLON
(ERRA EPOS)*

ERRA,‡ Rise up and march forth!
Like a pale old man, you linger in the city.
Like a crying child, you linger in the house...
Arise, hero! Ride the plains!
All man and beast shall lay low.
The gods will hear and dismay.
The kings will hear and be afraid.
The demons will hear and be terrified.
The mighty among men will hear and quake.
The towering mountains shall hear and tremble.
The wide sea will hear and be swept away.
ERRA, hear this! I have said the words!
Taut is the bow and sharp is the arrow!
The sword is drawn out for slaughter!
ERRA called to his Torch, his vizier, ISHUM:
"Open the path to me, I wish to take the road.
SIBBI, the hero unrivaled, will march at my side.
And, you *Ishum*, my guide,
Shall guard [walk] behind me."
ISHUM was saddened at these words.
ISHUM took pity and said: "Lord ERRA,
Against God and King you have planned evil,
To destroy all the world you have planned,
To destroy all the world is an evil plan.
Will you not turn back?"

---
* Mardukite Catalogue = *Tablet V*
‡ *Erra*—alternate name for *Nergal* in this cycle; meaning "annihilator."

ERRA opened his mouth to ISHUM:
"Silence, you, ISHUM, You, listen to me!
I will tell you of *humans* and their fate.
My guide—guide to the *gods*,
You, ISHUM, hear my words:
'In the heavens I am a wild ox, and on earth,
  the lion and on land, a king.
Among the gods, I am mighty, among the IGIGI,
I am valiant, among ANUNNAKI, I am powerful.
Because *humans* did not fear my words,
And heeded the words of MARDUK, but acted
  according to my heart,
I will arouse MARDUK, the princely one,
I will summon him forth from his home, and I will
  destroy *man*.'"
ERRA set his face toward BABYLON,
To the gates of BABYLON he set his feet.
ERRA planted his feet in BABYLON,
The City of MARDUK, King of the Gods.
To the ESAGILA, Home of Marduk, ERRA
  entered.
To MARDUK, the god, ERRA spoke:
"My Lord, the *nimbus*, the symbol of your
  lordship in BABYLON,
Exceeding in brightness, like a heavenly star, now
  darkened is its light.
The crown of your kingship in BABYLON, has
  been cast down.
March away from your dwelling-place,
Leave your people, your shrine-temple,
And set your face to the west, to the mountains of

the gods,
The fire that purifies your garments."
MARDUK, Lord of BABYLON, to ERRA said:
"If I leave BABYLON, my legacy on earth will be destroyed.
If I leave BABYLON, my home in the E.SAGILA, great chaos will rise up on earth.
The Evil Winds, the Evil Demons and Evil Spirits of the Underworld,
They will rise up and devour the living.
All living creatures on earth will the kill, with none to turn them back."
ERRA responded to MARDUK:
"That is why I have come, my Lord.
To take care of things in your absence.
I promise that none shall suffer in wake.
I will see to it that neither beast nor field is harmed.
No harm shall come to the earth, whether by *heavenly gods* or *Underworld demons*.
To this I promise, my Lord MARDUK."
MARDUK left through the Gates of BABYLON.
To maintain his lordship in BABYLON, MARDUK left for the god-mountain.
When the god was no longer seen from the heights of the E.SAGILA,
ERRA called to ISHUM:
"Open the gate, for I am leaving on the road,
The day has come and the hour is passed;
I will speak and the sun will drop its rays before me,

I will cover the darkness with the face of the day;
He who was born on the day of rain, shall be
 buried on a day of thirst.
He who went forth on a fertile path, will return on
 a road of barren dust.
I speak unto the 'king of the gods':
'Come forth not from the house you entered,
Faithfully I will carry out your commands;
When the Babylonians (*Akkadians*) cry out to you,
 O Lord,
Do not hear their prayers!'
I will put an end to all habitation, their homes
 turned to barren mounds.
I will empty out all of the cities, and turn them into
 ghostly ruins.
I will destroy the mountains and its life, the flocks
 and grazing beasts slain.
I will cause the seas to convulse, and destroy the
 fertility it brings.
I will uproot the marsh and the forest, and crush
 the mighty existences.
I will lay *humans* down, and annihilate all living
 creatures."
ISHUM stood by and listened to ERRA speak the
 doom of *humanity*.
ISHUM became filled with pity for *humanity* and
 said:
"Lord ERRA, Against God and King you have
 planned evil,
To destroy all the world you have planned,
To destroy all the world is an evil plan.

Will you not end this horror?"
ERRA listened not.
ERRA first stopped the 'waters' in BABYLON.
He then emptied the homes of BABYLON.
He then emptied the streets of BABYLON.
He then brought down the walls of BABYLON.
He then brought down the gates of BABYLON.
He then annihilated the fields of BABYLON.
He then annihilated the people of BABYLON.
ERRA stood and looked at his work.
Satisfied with the destruction of BABYLON,
ERRA planted his gaze toward ERECH saying:
"I am coming for you ERECH;
ERECH, the wicked city of *sinners*;
ERECH, the evil city of *sodomites*;
ERECH, the awful city of *eunuchs* in service to
  INANNA-ISHTAR;
ERECH, the lustful city of sacred *prostitutes*,
  whose husbands are the merrymakers of
  EANNA, temple-shrine of INANNA."
[*tablet break*]... leaving ERECH, now in ruin,
ERRA still felt no peace, no rest, saying in his
  heart:
"I shall slaughter the multitudes with a vengeance.
I shall kill the *son*, and the *father* will have to bury
  him.
I shall kill the *father* and there shall be *none* to
  bury him.
Whoever has made themselves a house, saying:
'This is my chamber of rest,
That I have made myself a place of peace,

When the spirits carry me at my death, here I will be laying.'
Him, I shall put immediately to death, destroying his chamber of rest.
And after it is ruined, I shall discard it to another."
ISHUM listened to this evil and was dismayed,
Pleading with ERRA saying:
"Mighty ERRA,
The righteous of the world you have put to death,
The unrighteous of this world you have put to death.
Those who have sinned, you have put to death,
And those who have not sinned, you have put to death.
Those who burned proper offerings to the *gods*,
You have put to death,
The king and his court, you have put to death.
The elders of the assemblies, you have put to death,
The young maidens and princes, you have put to death.
And yet you refuse to rest and find peace,
You stand their saying to your heart:
'I shall crush the mighty and lay low the weak.
I shall slay the leader and his host, and make the hosts turn back.
I shall destroy the tower and wall,
And remove the wealth of the city.
I shall rip out the mast, and the ship will be lost.
I shall break its beams, and it will not reach the shore.

I shall tear apart its cables, and shred its flag.
I shall empty the breast, and so the baby shall
  not live.
I shall dry up all the springs, and so the river will
  yield no fertility.
I shall make the planets fall from the sky,
And so the stars will be untended.
I shall tear out the roots of the trees,
And so no fruits shall grow.
I shall rip out the foundations,
And so the walls of all cities crumble.
To the home of the King of the Gods, I shall take
  for my own.
There is none that can oppose me!'"
The mighty ERRA listened to ISHUM.
The words of ISHUM soothed his heart.
He considered the Akkadians of BABYLON
And gave a moment of hope for *humanity*, saying:
"The Sealander and the Subaraen;
The Assyrian and the Elamite;
The Kassite and the Sutaen;
The Gutaen and the Lullamaen;
Land and City;
House will attack House;
Brother will not spare Brother;
They will all kill one another – and then
Will the Akkadians rise up and subdue them all!"
These words found ERRA and ISHUM at rest.
The anger toward *humanity* now soothed in the
  heart of ERRA.
Evil destruction; total annihilation; the wicked

Mountain:
"I am the voice of the God who cannot be here.
 am the voice of the God who is in the hearts of
  all men.
 am the voice of the God who appears in many
  faces.
 is I, the voice of the God, that will teach you the
  way,
nd I command you, dear son, to write this what I
  say on tablets for all of humanity's sake,
at they might honor the ANUNNAKI Gods of
  heir Ancestors,
 worship the Eternal Source of All Being &
  reation.
 not only the voice of your God, but also your
  ommander.
 are for the long and hard battle such as lies
  ead."
 U asked MARDUK:
  at can men do to prepare for the sake of their
   lives,
   can they live to serve and worship proper?"
   he voice of MARDUK echoed out:
    piously by the Code of the ANUNNAKI
    ets of Destiny.
    ere is no longer any religion higher than the
    ce.
    e desire of God is for us to love one
    er,
    t to sacrifice the life which has been made
    le.

plan did ISHUM end!
To peaceful ISHUM did ERRA speak:
"The people of the land, now few, will again turn to many.
Both short and tall will set to the roads.
The Akkadians will capture over the mighty.
To BABYLON the treasures will be restored.
The irate gods of the land, now appeased,
Will again come into their dwellings.
Cattle and grain will again prosper in the lands.
The fields which have now been laid desolate,
They will make again to earn produce.
All of the mighty, from all of the cities,
Will pay tribute to BABYLON.
The E.KUR and temples now destroyed, like the rising sun,
Their peaks shall shine forth again!
The Tigris and the Euphrates—
  they will overflow with fertile waters.
And unto the *End of Days*,
A New Babylon will *rule all the world!*"

EPILOGOS OF ISHUM (ERRA EPOS)*

I, ISHUM, account for these words, I have set them down on this tablet.
For the glory of ERRA, I have set down this song.
May it be sung until the *End of Days* to my Lord.
I have set down my account of my Lord, and how he became angry with *humans*.
I have shown his name to be the devastati[on of] lands.
I have revealed the evil plan to blot out th[e] existence of all *humanity*.
And how the soothing words of I, ISHU[M,] have brought peace to the heart of my [Lord.]
How ISHUM, his counselor, did pacify [   ] in his Lord's heart;
And how a remnant of hope was save[d]
For the *god* MARDUK and his son N[ABU, the] Tablet-Keeper.
I reveal these things to you as a *visi[on,]*
And when I had awoken from this d[ream,]
I set it down for you—
Without changing a word or a line [   ]

THE FIRST TABLET OF [

And so NABU {indicated as "I"} [   ] Mountain‡
To hear the Voice of the Great [God of the] Mountain.
To the Unseen God, whose vi[sion came] to the prophet.
And the voice of MARDUK [   ]

---

* Mardukite Catalogue = *Tablet V*

* Mardukite Catalogue = *Tabl[et VI]*
‡ The "pyramid" that Marduk [   ] punishment—in some vers[ions   ] destruction of Babylon; in [   ] death (drowning) of *Ishta[r]*

A certain knowledge of what is good and evil on Earth,
With perfected choice will be the former, so is the will of God.
There is no pleasure to be gained from the wasteful shed of blood.
Celebrate life and sing praises to the creation around you,
Which has been carefully made for you, by the Highest,
Under who the ANUNNAKI live and reign over the Lower."

And NABU asked MARDUK:

"For what can men do to repent of their sins if not by sacrifice?"

The voice of MARDUK responded:

"Give to the Eternal Source dedication and commitment in life,
And this is all that is asked of you in this life.
Men approach the face of God in fear and beg forgiveness,
When their efforts could be better spent in prayer and praise.
Men flood the temple-shrines with more food than is consumed,
When it could be better distributed among the poor.‡
Bring the God of Life no more vain offerings of

---

‡ Something later instilled by true Mardukite Babylonian Kings.

flesh.
Pray and live a pious life at one with creation.
How hard is this?
Make simple rituals if it pleases you,
For only prayer and devotion is asked of the God of All.
Do not deny yourself of a happy existence in the name of God.
Never let your livelihood be neglected because you worship the Highest.
Lives dedicated to the Source are not preoccupied by worship,
For to go out and act, live and demonstrate the pious life among men is best."

THE SECOND TABLET OF NABU-TUTU[*]

All things that are, are moved;
Only that which is not, is unmovable.
Every Body is changeable.
Not every Body is able to be dissolved into elements.
Some Bodies are able to be dissolved into elements.
Every living thing is not mortal.
Not every living thing is immortal.
That which may be dissolved is also corruptible.
That which is Eternal is unchangeable, incorruptible.

---

[*] Mardukite Catalogue = *Tablet T*

That which is unchangeable is eternal.
That which is always physical is always corrupted.
That which is made but once,
Is never corrupted and does not become any other thing.
First, God; Second, the World; Third, Man.
The World for Man, Man for God.
Of the Soul-Program:
That part has been given as the conscience of mortals,
But that which is Reasonable is immortal.
Every essence is immortal.
Every essence is unchangeable.
Every thing that is, is double: alpha and beta.
None of the things that are stand still.
Not all things are moved by a Soul-Program,
But everything that is, is controlled by its own Soul-Program.
Every thing that suffers is Sensible,
Every thing that is Sensible suffers.
Every thing that is sad is also able to rejoice,
And must be a mortal living Creature.
Not every thing that is able to be joyous can also be sad,
Like unto the eternal living things.
Not every Body can be sick;
  but every sick Body is dissoluble.
The Mind resides in the All [God].
Reasoning in experience is in Man,
Experience becomes the Reason in the Mind.
The Mind is void of suffering.

No thing in a Body is true.
All that is incorporeal, is void of untruth.
Every thing that is made is corruptible.
Nothing good made upon Earth, nothing evil made in Heaven.
God is good, Man is evil.
Good is voluntary, or of its own accord.
Evil is involuntary or against its will.
The Gods choose good things, as good things.
Time is a Divine [*Alpha*] thing;
  Law is Human [*Beta*].
Malice is nourishment of the Material Kingdom.‡
Time is the Corruption of Man.
Whatsoever is in Heaven is unalterable.
All upon Earth is alterable.
Nothing in Heaven is for a charge, nothing on Earth is free.
Nothing unknown in Heaven, nothing known upon Earth.
The things upon Earth communicate not with those in Heaven.
All things in Heaven are without blame,
All things upon Earth are subject to consequence.
That which is immortal, is not mortal:
That which is mortal is not immortal.
That which is sown, is not always brought to fruition;
But that which is manifest had always been sown.
Of the perishable Body, there are two Times,

---

‡   *Material Kingdom* = "*Physical Universe.*"

One from sowing to generation, one from
  generation to death.
Of an everlasting Body, the time is only from the
  Generation.
Perishable Bodies are increased and diminished,
Perishable matter is divided into contraries;
As in Corruption and Generation, but Eternal
  matter exists unto its self.

THE THIRD TABLET OF NABU-TUTU[*]

The Generation of Man is Corruption,
The Corruption of Man is the beginning of
  Generation.
That which off-springs or produces another,
Is itself an product of another.
Of things that are, some are in Bodies, some in
  their Ideas.
Whatsoever things belong to operation or working,
  are in a Body.
That which is immortal, partakes not of that which
  is mortal.
That which is mortal, does not come into an
  immortal Body,
But that which is immortal can come into a mortal
  Body.
Operations or Workings are not carried upwards,
But descend downwards.
Things upon Earth do nothing to advantage those

---

[*] Mardukite Catalogue = *Tablet T*

in Heaven,
But all things in Heaven can do profit
And advantage for the things upon Earth.
Heaven is capable and a fit receptacle of everlasting Bodies,
The Earth is one of corruptible Bodies.
The Earth is brutish, the Heaven is rational.
Those things that are in Heaven are subject or placed under it,
But the things on Earth, are placed over it's matrix
Heaven is the first Element; Providence is Divine Order.
Necessity is the Minister or Servant of Providence.
Fortune is the vehicle or consequence of what is without Order;
The focus of operation,
Nothing more than opinionated glamour or a fantasy.
Avoid all conversation, both idle and wise,
With the multitudes or common people of the masses,
For that which is Above
Would not have you become either the subject of Envy,
Much less to be considered ridiculous by the many.
The like have always been pulled toward themselves,
To that which is like,
Such as when the waters settle upon their levels.
The unlike will never agree with the unlike

natures,
Such is the pattern of their way:
Such as you will find
With the variegated philosophical discourses.
And dogmatic treatise that circulate among the masses.
The unlike natures are unique in one facet:
That they act as a sharpening stone for the evil tendencies in men,
Another vehicle for their maliciousness.
Conclusively it is better to avoid the multitudes
And realize that they are not in the path of understanding the virtue
And power of the things that have been said here.
And concerning the nature
And composition of those living things called "Humans,"
It may be simply said that they are prone to maliciousness, being something they are both familiar with and nourished by.
When first the world was made,
All things were in perfected accordance
With Providence and Necessity, Destiny [or Fate],
Bearing Rule over all. Knowing this perfection,
The mortal creatures will be the worse for it,
Despising the whole because it was made.
And if the only power known to them is to be the evil cause
Of disorder upon Fate or Destiny,
Than they will never abstain from the tendencies
Toward evil doings.

PRELUDE TO CHALDEO-ASSYRIAN BABYLON (KING-LISTS)[*]

A reformed BABYLON[†] began with the ISIN Dynasty:

MARDUK-KABIT-AHESHU [9 yr], ITTI-MARDUK-BALATU [15 yr], NINURTA-NADIN-SHUMI [6 yr], NABU-KUDURRI-USUR [23],[‡]
ENLIL-NADIN-APLI [3 yr] and MARDUK-NADIN-AHHE [18 yr], MARDUK-SHAPIK-ZERI [13 yr] and ADAD-APLA-IDDINA [23 yr],
MARDUK-AHHE-ERIBA [1 yr] and MARDUK-ZERX [13 yr], NABU-SHUM-LIBUR [7 yr] and SIMBAR-SHIPAK [28 yr], EA-MUKIN-SHUMI [1 yr] and KASHU-NADIN [4 yr], EULMA-SHAKIN-SHUMI [16 yr], NINURTA-KU-DURI ASUR [2 yr], SHIRIQTI-SHUQAMUNU [1 yr]
And MAR-BITI-APLA-ASUR [6 yr], NABU-MUKIN-APLI [36 yr] and NINURTA-KUDURRI-ASUR [1 yr], MAR-BITI-AHHE-IDDINA [23 yr]
And SAMAS-MUDAMMIQ [20 yr], NABU-SHUMA-UKIN [12 yr] and NABU-APLA-IDDINA [33 yr], MARDUK-ZAKIR-SHUMI [36 yr], MARDUK-BALASSU-IQBI [5 yr], BABA-AHA-IDDINA [2 yr].

And then five kings in five years followed by

---

[*] Mardukite Catalogue = *Tablet K*
[†] Presumably c. 12th Century B.C.
[‡] Also known as *Nebuchadnezzar I*, not to be confused with the famous Neo-Babylonian King *Nebuchadnezzar II*.

NINURTA-APLAX [10 yr] and MARDUK-BEL-
ZERI [10 yr], MARDUK-APLA-ASUR [12 yr] and
ERIBA-MARDUK [8 yr],
NABU-SHUMA-ISHKUR [12 yr] and NABUNAS-
IR [14 yr], NABU-NADIN-ZERI [2 yr] and
NABU-SHUMA-UKIN II [1 yr]
Before the emergence of the (10th) Dynasty,‡ under
NABU-MUKINZERI, NABU-MUKIN-ZERI ruled
[2 yr] in BABYLON and
Then TIGLATH-PILESAR III [2 yr] and SHAL-
MANESSAR [5 yr], MARDUK-APLA-IDDINA I
[12 yr],† SARGON II [SHARRUKIN II] [5 yr] and
SENNA-CHERIB [2 yr], MARDUK-ZAKIR-
SHUMI II and MARDUK APLA-IDDINA II
shared 1 year,
BEL-IBNI [2 yr] and ASHUR-NADIN-SHUMI [6
yr], NERGAL-[M]USHEZIB [2 yr] and MUSHEZ-
IB-MARDUK [4 yr],
Who was ruling when the ASSUR dominated
BABYLON for a time.
The Assyrian, ASSURBANIPAL, ruled 21 years
And SAMAS-SUMA-UKIN at the same,
KANDALANU also ruled 21 years; SINSUMLISIR
only 1.
The 21 year reign of NABU-APLA-ASSUR
[NEBOPOLASSAR] brought the new (neo)
dynasty [Chaldean] to rule in BABYLON,
Followed by NABU-KUDURRI-ASUR

---

‡ Presumably c. 8th Century B.C.
† Possibly one of the Judeo-Christian "*biblical
Merodach*" figures.

[NEBUCHADNEZZAR II] [42 yr], AMAL-MAR-
DUK [2 yr] and NERGAL-SHAR-ASUR [4 yr],
LABASHI-MARDUK [1 yr] and NABUNAID(US)
[17 yr],
Who was ruling when CYRUS [9 yr] launched the
Persian Empire in BABYLON

THE NEBUCHADNEZZAR II TABLET*

Lord MARDUK, Glorious Chief of the
ANUNNAKI has heard my petition.
Lord MARDUK, Captain among the ANUNNAKI
has received my prayer.
I have subdued those who do not heed to the Will
of MARDUK.
I have overcome the rebels in the country, and
made the inhabitants of my kingdom
Loyal through their prosperity.
To BABYLON, I have carried Gold, Silver,
Copper, Lapis Lazuli
And other precious stones and expensive woods
[resins] from the mountains.
I have decorated the Shrine of MARDUK,
The ESAGILA, Shrine of MARDUK, I have
decorated with gold.
Wood from the finest cedars of LEBANON
comprise the roof.
And I have decorated the "Boat" of MARDUK.
The Gate of NANNA-SIN, I have plated with

---

* Mardukite Catalogue = *Tablet L*

fine Silver.
The AIBURSHABU,[‡] I have paved with tiles.
Since MARDUK created me to be king,
And NABU has culled his people to my realm,
As the love I have for my own life,
So do I feel toward the building and reign of their cities.

A DRAGON-KING'S PRAYER TO MARDUK[*]

O Lord MARDUK, Prince of the Gods,
You who created me to be king among your people,
And committed the hearts of the people to my sovereignty.
As my life, I love the supremacy of your cities.
No other city exists in the world such as is your home.
In honor of your godhead, I seek the power of your lordship.
May the house I have made your shrine endure for all eternity,
Just as you shall endure.
MARDUK, compassionate one among the Highest,
May I be satisfied by your fullness and may I reach long prosperous years.
May my offspring be blessed.

[‡] The processional "way" or avenue leading to *Marduk's* temple-shrine.

[*] Mardukite Catalogue = *Tablet L*

May the true Dragon-Kings who rule over all mankind
Bring tribute to the name of MARDUK.
In his midst may I too receive tribute,
From the foundations of the Heavens to its heights,
From the rising Sun to its setting,
May I possess no foes and may I gain no enemies.
In the words of Truth, I speak.
And may the posterity of Dragonblood
Rule over the lands of Men, forever and ever.

THE CAPTURE OF BABYLON WITH THE FAVOR OF MARDUK (CYRUS)*

I, CYRUS, was sought out by MARDUK.
MARDUK sought me, a righteous prince,
A worthy king to take the Hand of MARDUK.
MARDUK proclaimed me "King of Anshan"
And the title "Lord of the World" he gave to me.
By divine right, upgraded with Dragonblood, I moved.
I moved on the land of KUTI and compelled them.
The men bowed to their king in the name of MARDUK.
The men were delivered into my hands by MARDUK,
And I governed with justice and righteousness.
MARDUK, the Great Lord, Protector of the

---

*   Mardukite Catalogue = *Tablet L*

People,
MARDUK smiled upon me [CYRUS] with joy.
To his city of BABYLON, the Great Lord bid me to move.
On the road to BABYLON, the Great Lord set me.
And MARDUK marched by my side as friend and counsel.
As we marched, our caravan increased in number.
Soldiers and arms in allegiance with MARDUK came.
But no war was to be fought.
The Road to BABYLON was opened before us.
Unopposed we marched to Gates of the city of BABYLON
And MARDUK demanded that his city would go unharmed.
Entering the city through the Gate of MARDUK,
The Great Lord demanded NABONIDUS be delivered to him,
A king who had not upheld the will of MARDUK.
CYRUS was made king before the grace of MARDUK.
The Babylonians, the people of SUMER and AKKAD,
The courtly princes and governors, every shepherd and peasant
Bowed to the sovereignty of MARDUK.
With bright faces the name of MARDUK was exalted
And equally to the power [reign] of CYRUS on Earth.

Lord MARDUK, who can raise the dead to life.
Lord MARDUK, remover of destruction and want.
Lord MARDUK, who has smiled on CYRUS.
CYRUS, the Mighty King of BABYLON.
CYRUS, the Great King of the Wind [Command].
CYRUS, the Powerful King of SUMER and AKKAD.
CYRUS, the Earthly King of the Four Quarters [of the world].
I [CYRUS] have entered BABYLON favorably,
And made my abode in the High Place,
In return for the daily devotion to the MARDUK.
By the command of Lord MARDUK,
Patron of the Babylonians,
I have restored the ANUNNAKI [gods] to their shrines,
And cast out the abominations conjured by NABONIDUS.
May all the ANUNNAKI [gods] whom have been restored [To their cities and shrines] pray daily to BEL-MARDUK and his son NABU,
For the lengthening of my days of reign,
And may they speak the words among the people
That which are prayers to my Lord, MARDUK:
"Let King CYRUS, who worshiped you properly,
And his son CAMBYSES, live long and prosperous lives."

THE PRIEST-KING'S TABLET OF WISDOM[*]

To the kings and priests is given the Tablet [of wisdom].
For the wise among men is given the True Words of Power.
To be wise is to be discreet in your undertakings,
Be humble in your knowledge, and guard that knowledge.
The wise does not speak needlessly, but carefully.
As you would closely guard riches, so your words.
Allow no arrogance or falsehood to come into your speech.
The wise first and foremost seek after the Truth.
Execute your actions in the Light of Truth,
Worship thy God daily with prayer and appropriate incense,
And with your heart obediently given to thy Lord, your God,
For such is the life acceptable unto God.
Blessed is the one who respects the ANUNNAKI,
For you shall enjoy prosperity.
Blessed is the one who offers food at the Altar of Sacrifices,
For you shall enjoy a long life.
Blessed is the one who leads a life of prayer,
For you shall enjoy freedom from sin.
Blessed is the one who worships with humble prostrations,

---

[*] Mardukite Catalogue = *Tablet L*

For you shall enjoy the graces of the ANUNNAKI.
Blessed is he who loves and honors the
 ANUNNAKI,
But does not dismiss the Infinite Source—your
 God,
For you shall enjoy Eternal Life in the Abode of
 Heaven.

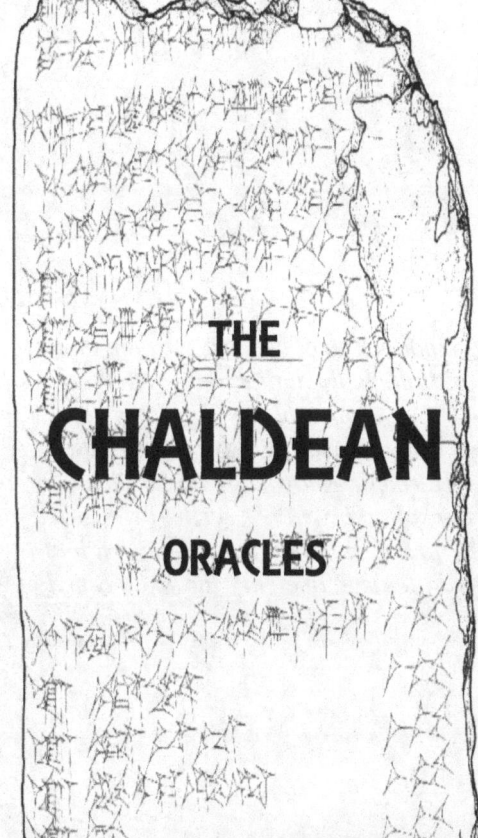

THE
CHALDEAN
ORACLES

*A collection of esoteric wisdom tablets
allegedly authored by "He Who
Contemplates The Stars"
and providing a synthesis of the
Hermetic Knowledge and Philosophy
inspired by Nabu's scribe-priests and
priestesses that upheld the original
traditions in ancient Mardukite Babylon.*

CHALDEAN ORACLES—TABLET I[*]
CAUSE, GOD. FATHER, MIND, FIRE.
MONAD, DYAD, TRIAD.

The voice of the God with the head of a hawk.
The God that is incorruptible, eternal, unbegotten, undivided,
The dispenser of all that is good and indestructible;
The best of what is good; The wisest of what is wise;
He is the Father of equality and justice,
He is the Father of the self-taught, physical, perfect and wise
Who know the meaning of these words and are inspired.
The magicians come forth knowing that he is the God,
And he is celebrated by his Older and Younger names,
Circulating through and about the Universe as the Eternal God,
Understanding the meaning of all numbers,
And the movements of all things in the Universe,
Which are infinite and flow through the spiral force.
The true and indestructible God is known as "Silence,"
By the Divine Powers of the Universe,

---

[*] Mardukite Catalogue = *Tablet O*

And is known to the souls of humans
Through the power of the Mind alone.
There are no speakable names for this force,
Though he has been known as IAO,‡
Signifying he is above the Seven Pillars of Material Existence.
The Father conceals himself, withdrawn from our sight.
He is enveloped in the Fire of the Intelligent Light.
The Mind was activated before energy permeated the Universe.
The Second Mind rules the "Empyrean World."†
Though power is with them, the Mind is from the One.
The Mind of the One soars with the guise of relentless fire.
After the paternal conception in the soul resides,
The heat resonates forth to animate all things.
The Intelligible was placed within Soul Programs,
And the Soul Programs were placed in dull bodies.
The Father of Gods and Men activated these Soul Programs.
Natural works co-exist with the Father's Intelligent Light.

---

‡ *IAO*—Greek Gnostic-Hermetic threefold (unspeakable or ineffable) "Name of God"; metaphysically equated to the Mardukite Zuist (and Systemology) concept of the *Abzu*, if we are speaking in purely Alpha-spiritual terms and not mythographic pantheism.

† "*Empyrean*"—Greek Hermetic term for "holy" or (heavenly) "Divine."

The Soul Program is dispensed from Heaven,
And the control of that program was established on high.
The Eternal Spark imbued is a brilliant never ceasing fire,
The Mistress of Life that fills the many recesses of the World.
And the fiery whirlwind drew forth all of its brilliance,
Resonating outward, penetrating the abysses of the Universe,
Extending to the material world, seven wondrous rays.
The monad first existed, and the paternal monad persists still.
When the monad divided itself, the dyad was generated.
The dyad glitters with Intelligible Light,
Spreading to govern all things [in lower orders]
And to give order to everything not ordered.
When the Father's Mind was further divided by Will,
The decree was put forth that the One shall be Three,
And when the Will was inserted into the Soul Program,
All things in material existence were so divided: Light, Mind and Will.
Every spirit and form in the Universe was governed as such.
The Eternal Spark was mingled from the triad.

And on the Ladder of Lights they are known as
The Three Supernals—governing the existence of the Seven.
The Force emanated the Three: Virtue, Wisdom and Ineffable Truth.

CHALDEAN ORACLES—TABLET II[*]
IDEAS, INTELLIGIBLES.
INTELLECTUALS, AIR.

The Father whirled forth by invincible Will and Thought formed.
The Fountain of Beginnings and Endings was sprung forth.
The Fountains sprung up—being divided, but were One.
By Intellectual Fire, The Fountain was distributed among the Intelligibles.
The Universe shined forth with Ideas in all forms.
But the primary Father poured forth the Primordial Idea (Prime Thought).
The Three Supernal Rays shinned forth.
And many ideas and rays shinned forth onto the world.
But all things are connected in the Intelligible World,
And the Seven are the Three and the Three are the One.
But the Intellect cannot exist without the

---

[*] Mardukite Catalogue = *Tablet O*

Intelligible.

By Intellect, the Intelligibles introduced the Souls into the World.

By Intellect, the Intelligibles introduced Senses into the World.

And the Paternal Intellect has distributed secret symbols within.

Those who have known the mysteries will reveal:

It is contained within Mystic Silence.

The whirlwinds of the ALL-Father give watch to the Supernals.

The properties of his own strength,

He mingled it with the Material Synod.

And there are many who serve the Synods.

The Fountain of Life was sprung forth by Blessed Intellectuals,

Who had first received their own powers from its waters.

It was poured forth to supply perpetual Generations of form.

The Fountains of the Intellectuals are bound the the "depths."

And there is the power and strength of its sections.

Oh how indeed the material world has inflexible Rulers.

The thunders and rolling fires are sprung forth,

And the Spirits of the Poles, fiery in nature, are kindled.

The Fountain of Fountains.

Like unto the One, but divided from the rest.

Under two Minds united, the life-generating

fountain flows.
Beneath is the *a priori* [Principle One] of the Immaterials.
The Fountains churn and the principles whirl, ceaseless.
The Principles of Principles,
Which have understood the Intelligible works of the Father,
He has given sensible bodies of form.
These energetic links allow the Father communicate with matter,
The symbols and images are immaterial,
Reflecting the natures of the unapparent matrix of this world.

CHALDEAN ORACLES—TABLET III[*]
POWERS. ORDERS, WATER.
SOULS, MAN, LIFE.

In the leaves of the Olden Book read in the Greek tongue:
TYPHON [TIAMAT], ECHIDNA and PYTHONI,
The progeny of TARTAROS and GAEA,
United by AN, forming the Supernal Triad of the Old Ones.
AN, Inspector General and Guardian of the chaotic fabrications.
To what are the natures of these material fabrications?

---

[*] Mardukite Catalogue = *Tablet O*

Irrational Daemons formed Mindless Elementals,
Their existence becomes dependent on the Aerial Rulers
The powers given to the Aerial, Terrestrial and Aquatic domains.
All intelligences are the ideas put forth from the ALL [Father],
And all the bodies contained the Divine Spark,
All mortal bodies were animated by the breath of the Source.
For the fractured mind and soul-programs
Were put into the crystalline networks [human bodies].
And within the containment of each is hidden the Soul-Symbol,
By which the ALL can recognize the Divine Spark
United from two substances: The Mind and the Divine Spirit,
And as to the third, a secret Perfect Holy Love,
The Venerable Charioteer that united the destiny of the Universe.
The life-giving power is imbued with the Breath and Mind,
But the Ineffable Love must be joined to create and for it to exit.
The spirit form was imbued with Divine Love.
And the Soul-Program enveloped the existence to itself,
As the ALL [Source] possessed nothing material or mortal,
And was whole within itself—by the Intelligent

Light.
The glories are to be experienced from within the mortal bodies.
Higher Powers are self-knowing.
Their power is the perception of self-honest Truth,
Through themselves, their thought-forms are more creative.
Such are bound by no deception,
And are able to survive the wall of fire by their own accord.
The Perfected Souls recognize the symbols of the Father
And understand their significance.
To ascend is to avoid the deterministic Wing of Fate;
To place the Will and Mind and Soul with God,
To return to the Source of All being and creation -
These are the light-bearers, the gate-keepers,
Those who have descended on Earth from Heaven,
To gather about the souls of "Empyrean Fruits"
Grown from the soul-nourishing flower of life.
The Soul-Program grew upon itself and became a Demon.
The *anima* [animistic] or pneumatic soul-stuff
Became an intelligent spirit unto itself,
And projected for itself the image of a disembodied form.
It is from this form that the soul punishes itself and is punished.
The Demon can create itself a realm to be miserable,

But the visions of being entrapped in "Hades" are self-created.
From one life to another, the soul-program passes,
Carried on the Union-Love of the Divine Spark,
To and from widely distributed places, passing above and below
And through the Center of the Earth [Existence],
And from the Middle Earth, passing its fiery center,
The life-bearing fires consume themselves, in the Depths of the Material World.
Water is the symbol of life.
The Soul-Program perpetually follows the Wheel of Destiny,
Compelled to repeat [recursive] upon itself,
The Dragon swallows its tail,
As does the Matrix of Creation that is the Physical World.
The travels of the spirit repeat unless the level is overcome.

CHALDEAN ORACLES—TABLET IV[*]
MATTER. WORLDLY NATURE, EARTH.

The Material World is upon a Matrix that contains all things.
The Material World is wholly divisible, and yet indivisible.
The aerial, astral, terrestrial and aquatic share the

---

[*] Mardukite Catalogue = *Tablet O*

domain.
Matter only pervades throughout the world of form,
And is the domain of the "Gods."
The Eternal Self-Created "Mind" is immaterial [beyond physical]
And it experiences itself through the experience of the parts.
The true nature of the Divine is "incorporeal" [without body],
And these are bound to bodies for you to have experience.
In this chain, the experience of the illusion of time,
All beings remain in the Light of the ALL [Father],
So that the Universe may continue in infinite time and love,
And the elemental forces of the Material World,
Will continue their course, and the wheel continues to spin.
The Physical forms are the fabrications of the Mind,
They imitate [mirror] the *a priori* [archetypal] Thought.
But these thoughts at first had no form to hold them.
The creation were brought forth by the Venerable Name,
Which was shouted and leaped out into the realms,
The fiery rapid tones of the ALL-Father resonating vibrations.
From the Astral Light, the lower visions appear in

the Physical Universe.
From the Astral comes the elemental realms of the Physical:
Fire, Air, Water, Earth and the all-encompassing Ether.‡
The Air was placed above the Middle Earth,
The Waters were placed below the Middle Earth,
And Fire was blended with the Stars and Fire was forced into StarFire.
The Seven Rays (Pillars) of the Firmaments of the Cosmos,
They circumscribed the heavens like a serpent,
Bound to the wandering gods [planets].
The disorder of the wandering gods was fixed,
To the stations [zonei] of the highway [ladder] they were fixed.
Six in number—the Seventh cast into the fiery sun.
The center of all is equal and harmonic to the One.
And even the swift-footed Sun must travel around a center.

---

‡ *"Ether"* or *"Æther"*—a term representing the unifying elemental quintessence or *"fifth element,"* also referred to by mystics as *"Akasha"* and often related to *"Zu"* in Mardukite Systemology.

CHALDEAN ORACLES—TABLET V*
MAGICAL PRECEPTS & AKASHA.

Do not fix your mind on the vast systems of the Earth;
For the Plant of Truth grows not upon the ground.
You need not measure the motions of the Sun,
Or collect rules for its travel,
For this is already done by the Eternal Will of the ALL Father,
And it is not for your sake on Earth to understand this Will.
Dismiss from your mind the necessity
To project the course of the Moon,
For the Celestial Orb moves always by the power of necessity.
The procession of the Stars and the Zodiac is a Godly thing
And was not generated in this world for your sake.
Observing the aerial flight paths of birds will give you no true knowledge,
Nor will the dissection of the entrails of your victims—
These are mere toys and the basis of fraudulent mediums.
Move, therefore, away from the Material World,
If you should enter the Star-Gate of the Sacred Paradise,
Where only Virtue, Wisdom and Unity are

---

* Mardukite Catalogue = *Tablet O*

assembled.
Stoop not, therefore, down unto this Darkly-Splendid World;
Wherein lies a continually faithless "depth"
And Hades[‡] shrouded in cloudy gloom,
Delighting in senseless images,
In a tortuous, winding, ever-rolling Abyss;
Containing the lightless body—formless and void.
Keep not to the path which is equal with the dross of Matter,
For there is a place for your Image that is much more splendid,
And it may be reached by first traveling past the Gate of Earth,
And then upon the *Ladder* which has *Seven Steps*,
Therein lies a Throne of a devastating and fatal force.
Invoke not the visible image of the Soul of Nature,
For the material world has but one name, which is Death.
To look upon and give to these is to be as one with them,
And they seduce the soul-programs from their progress,
Whereby they may be kept from the sacred mysteries.
There is only one sin: To defile the Divine Spark within.

[‡] This tablet translation comes from Greek-language Hermetics.

Do not change the barbarous Names of Evocation,
For they are sacred names in every language,
And they have been entrusted to you by the God,
Who renders all the powers of the Sacred Rites possible.
It would be wise to hasten yourself onto the Ladder of Lights,
To become a receptacle for the Seven Rays of the Father.
Seek Paradise—Return to the Source.
Things Divine are not attainable by mortals
Who understand [by] the body alone,
But only by those who approach the Eternal Fire,
Submitting themselves in self-annihilation.
Fortify and purify your soul, make it ready to be a beacon of Light,
Embodied by the Seven Rays, that are Three, that are One.
Your Goddess will furnish you with every kind of armor.
Let that which is in your center,
The Divine Spark of the ALL-Father Source
Guide you on the Ladder of Lights.
Keep watch of the gates—plant your gaze always upward.
You who discovers the Absolute Truth of your own nature,
Shall be revealed the truth of all things—
For that which you experience comes first from within you.
The one who does not recognize—will be

fruitlessly vigilant.
So therefore, first, the Priest who governs the
works of Fire,
Must sprinkle about the Waters of the loud-
resounding Sea.
Should you see a terrestrial demon approach –
Scream at it!
If you invoke the lower often, the darkness will
consume you.
You will no longer see the Intelligent Light,
And you will no longer be visible to the Light-
Bearers,
Who suspend themselves from the vaulted sky of
Heaven,
Then will three lightning bolts strike,
And all things will be engulfed in chaotic
thunders.
Then comes the Fire,
Flashing and extending through the rushes of
the Air,
Or a fire most formless, which carries the Vision
and the Voice,
Or a flashing light, abounding, revolving, whirling
forth
And crying aloud.
Behold a vision of the flashing Light-Bearer, or a
boy king,
Who has been carried on the fiery celestial steed,
And is clothed in fire and gold and shoots bolts
from his bow,
While standing on the shoulders of the horse.

If you can sustain your meditation to this point still,
You will behold these symbols united in the form of a lion.
There is an Incorruptible Flame above the Celestial Lights,
Always sparkling, the Spring of Life, the Formation of all Beings,
The original archetype [First Form] of all things.
This flame produces all things,
And no existence may perish except what it consumes.
This flame cannot be contained in any single place
And it encompasses the Starry Heavens you can see.
Whosoever understands the meaning of these things;
Shall not experience death.

THE
SAJAHA
ORACLES

*A collection of Babylonian wisdom tablets
authored by "Sajaha-the-Seer-of-Marduk"
—a high priestess in the Temple of Marduk
during the reign of Nebuchadnezzar II—
including her prophetic visions of
a New Babylon Rising...*

THE SAJAHA SERIES – TABLET I[*]

1. Sajaha—My king, as you already know, there are vibrations and energy flows of different types and strength; everywhere and in everything and in everyone.

2. For everything and also for all people, there exists a permanent force in a sea of cosmic and magical vibrations and energy currents; equal to a large lake, which is composed of many different seas in itself.

3. And so everything emerges from and everyone experiences reality from oceans of vibrations and energetic flows that incessantly emits a field and also reproduces by itself; but without ability to determine anything about any of these things—often without even noticing.

4. It is participation in *games* of vibration and energy currents that challenge everyone to maintain a high degree of purity to remain close to the Source of All Being—the *All-as-One*—from which people have become almost entirely lost since the demise of the original empire. And the intermingling descendants lost most of the old power.

5. It has come to be—in times being what they are—especially in that which pertains to the subtle vibrating Force flowing unobserved, that powers are directed only to a small extent of their potential,

---

[*] Mardukite Catalogue = *Tablet S*

never really mastered or used conveniently.

6. This resulted due to the nerve-qualities of the ancestors, necessary for mastery of high power—Divine Right on Earth—being diluted among the descendants today and the pure descendants of these forces are no longer among the population.

THE SAJAHA SERIES – TABLET II[*]

1. Ereshkigal—Oh, wise one. Where did the district get its start? And whence comes its end?

2. Where the light ends, is the beginning of the circle, and where darkness ends, there is an end.

3. Because it all began in light, travels through the darkness, and returns to light.

4. From the knowledge of eternity-in-infinity, I have drawn a circle with my stylus on a stone. What is the meaning of this?

5. Everything is in that world, which also applies in this one—and there are still a thousand times more.

6. The circle marked shows nothing more than a small image of the *Great All*.

7. What makes one thing different from another? How is the circle at the beginning and end of [All] this!

---

[*] Mardukite Catalogue = *Tablet S*

8. They are the beginning and the end; one as the other.

9. Whatever you start in the earth world is not separate; it significantly and necessarily has its higher counterpart in the *Otherworld*.

10. By drawing the circle with the stylus on the stone, a self-contained line is demonstrated, according to its kind, neither beginning nor ending and yet we can behold its existence!

11. So it is with the great cycle of eternity-in-infinity: eternally connected is *All-as-One* from the beginning to the end.

12. This indicates that now everything is inseparable from the beginning to the end, unsolvable by all cycles of eternity. And as you know your circle drawn not distinguish the beginning and end, as is what happens to the *Source-of-All-Being*.

13. The breath of eternity is *All-as-One*; the beginning is familiar and the perceived end is the end of the beginning.

14. If you do not comprehend these things now, then go and experience more in the *Otherworld*.

THE SAJAHA SERIES – TABLET III[*]

1. Sajaha—Much has been, much will be, and in between what has been and what will be coming,

---
[*] Mardukite Catalogue = *Tablet S*

is the *kNow*.

2. But this *kNow* is but always only a half-breath, and there is no scale by which to measure it.

3. MARDUK, surveyor of everything, who added to the people's knowledge, the *kNow*, the power of eternity-in-infinity.

4. MARDUK sees the beginning and the end. In between, he sees the people on earth, they can not believe what they behold of the gods.

5. The people are the shadows of the gods. They act at their own discretion on earth. Their inheritance in the Light is to blame; for it is the seed of Darkness.

6. MARDUK sets forth the way of the walking for the *Seekers*. Choose your path and guide the people.

7. The compassionate eye of MARDUK gazes upon an erring race, creation of the gods. He shines upon the right way to go. He gives advice only. The *Seeker* is never forced on the path.

8. This is now the way of things—a way best likened to the spider's web. It is always difficult to find only the most direct path.

THE SAJAHA SERIES – TABLET IV[*]

1. Sajaha – From the dreams that come at night, I will speak to you of strange things. The Night wants you to discover strange things.

2. Dreams come as different types. There are dreams that allow you to walk in the *dreamscape*. There are dreams that bring you to another person. There are also dreams that make you feel different afterward. And there are dreams that quickly disappear from consciousness.

3. There are some things you see more clearly in sleep [*dreams*], which is merely a shadow [reflection] of the light of day. Such is not so much a "dream" as it is a composition of [resonant] images from the (surface) world.

4 But if in sleep, the inner [*alpha*] body is lifted from the outer, then you have dreams.

5. Because it is so that the inner body is linked back to the *alpha* state, the outer (surface) world, the *afterbirth*, is here and now All-as-One in the world. The cloak of form is temporary and hence, sleep.

6 And so then the spirit leaves the earthly body during rest and relaxation. Sometimes the spirit seeks out another human simulacrum whose vibration is similar to his, and moves temporarily into

---

[*] Mardukite Catalogue = *Tablet S*

this. If you find you do (have experienced) much in your dreams, then all this happened.

7. But it can also happen the other way around—that the spirit of another sleeper joins with yours. This conjures mental images of another person's life mixed with your own. Although it may seem confusing, all of the images are true in their own way.

8. But these dreams are merely the smaller of possible avenues. There are larger more important ones; if the entirety of your [*alpha*] spirit unveils its worldly glamour completely and enters into the world of sleep. There are numerous spiritual encounters taking place with each other while sleeping. How else are the images you remember upon awakening often entirely foreign to you.

9. Another [*dream*] avenue can lead to the limits of the *Grassland* [*Summerland*]— and perhaps even to a specific place there. Then your mind will have experienced much in the hours of sleep—via the far reaches of the eyes of the [*alpha*] spirit.

10. From the point of the [*alpha*] spirit as *Observer*, he sees the essence of the earthly [*physical*] world in (*self-honest*) truth; nothing is hidden from him; all thoughts are laid before him; the veil of glamour is lifted. And what you realize you from there, is that which is truly valuable knowledge.

11. But it can also be the case that when your body is sleeping dormant and you make leave of your own mind, that strange (foreign) spirits might temporarily take hold of the simulacrum. Such happens when the [*alpha*] spirit is not strong enough to complete protective circuit of the (earthly) body against the invasion of the strange (foreign). And everywhere danger lurks.

12. Everything that you see in (real) dreams are really alive somewhere. Nothing is mere unfounded illusion.

13. The mind, due to its own nature, does not look for random paths; it seeks what it lacks. It *craves* to *kNow*.

14. You may awaken from your dreams confused, feeling that the you that is you is not true, or you may only partially remember several dreams that you had.

15. And Everything is connected together sharing spirit, dreams, and even areas where the mind does not comprehend—at animal and plant vibrations.

16. All things are connected—*All-as-One*...

THE SAJAHA SERIES – TABLET V[*]

1. Sajaha – Through the astral [*stars*] sky I flew like an eagle in the azure blue night, which is a different night than the night of the earth, and constantly endures [*as the astral or starry sky*].

---
[*] Mardukite Catalogue = *Tablet S*

2. I learned to control my [*astral*] wings; nowhere and everywhere—at once—I found the boundary. I beheld the earthly [*physical*] world in a torrential sea of currents—such as you do not see from this *side*, which is not so much looked upon but *felt*: You were there—*All-as-One*—and your [*alpha*] spirit came down to the earthly [*physical*] world, and embraced the *genetic vehicle* occupied, and have kept your survival there/here as the necessary basis for life/awareness.

3. The image before me showed the earthly [*physical*] world not so large, and the stars were not so small, and while many were similar, they were all different from each other. There were [*star*] worlds red and yellow, blue and green, white and also those of nearly black. There were others of variegated colors. Some radiate such intense light out of themselves that I could not perceive their form. Others were of a different kind altogether of which I have no words to describe.

4. I beheld a vision of the sun, that which shone down upon the earth; bright and hot and glowing like gold. Then, I saw the moon, ruler of the night as it would seem from Earth. All about I saw the earth [*physical*] world suspended on imperceptible strings—like the sun's rays.

5. And the vibrations carried me back through sparkling lights and darkness—in alternation – and I do not know where. And then I saw another earth-like world; both familiar and yet alien at the same time. I descended. The sky was a bluish red, and there was no daylight other than this moonlight formed by the luminance of two moons.

6. Then a storm whirled and spun me around, and my hair caught in the vibrations and then it ceased to roar and was quieted. I floated home, past other worlds: the night, the dark, the blue, took me back.

7. Now I am standing on the summit of the temple and extend my gaze upward into the night. It is very quiet...

THE SAJAHA SERIES – TABLET VI[*]

1. Sajaha—I beheld visions of demons waiting at the edge of a grassland. ENLIL crouched before the legion of evil spirits begging for assistance against the kingdom of MARDUK, inciting battle among the [*ilu*] gods.

2. But the demons paid no attention.

3. The Prince of Shadows, in his gloom, thirsts for blood as refreshment, corruption as enjoyment.

4. I have bore witness to the evil spirits descending in swarms upon the earthly [*physical*] world; to stir up evil, according to their nature; instilling hatred in weak minds and sowing murder in weaker ones; giving rage-filled cups to the thirsting

---

[*] Mardukite Catalogue = *Tablet S*

nations to drink from—inciting warfare everywhere.

5. I beheld visions of demons lingering at the border of this world. Some forming an alliance with ENLIL—disaster threatens the people of Earth. Some carrying the rage-filled cups to the people, thereby made drunk and reeling in belligerence and delusion...

6. The servants of evil are evil—they are emissaries of your harm.

7. I have beheld baneful images of things to come: emissaries of your harm—the evil spirits—gain power on Earth.

8. Things most horrific are to come and conditions will worsen until finally the spirit of the righteous (*sword*) awakens and takes control of *New Babylon*: the pure mound—the bright place—to shatter the darkness...

THE SAJAHA SERIES – TABLET VII*

1. Sajaha—A gray cloud creeps closer upon us, but it bears no rain. They do not produce a gentle shade; it obscures the Light in totality.

2. It displeases me to report that a driven Darkness approaches for the coming times. The temples burst apart and the overtake kings. The people

---

* Mardukite Catalogue = *Tablet S*

succumb to jealousy—envy fuels hatred—hatred feeds forces of evil; and everywhere war erupts.

3. It displeases me to report that I see no beautiful light. For the Light that will come swirled in confusion and chaos that confounds the people—on the backs of slain servants of Darkness.

4. They will mix the Light from the slain servants of darkness with wrong [*notes*].

5. And the gray cloud pushes closer. They cluster together and darken the sky everywhere over the world.

6. And then the majority of the people of earth no longer distinguish between black and white; clueless, they confuse the natures of good and evil and blindly reel in their own delusions. But... *nothing is permanent; everything falls apart*.

7. I am pleased to report only one thing: that the seventh race of humans will rise again in the future, having first purged all souls of the people of earth; when the truth that nothing is separate—*All-as-One*.

THE SAJAHA SERIES – TABLET VIII[*]

1. Sajaha—I behold visions of angry faces that appear and melt away. They are not demons; they do

---

[*] Mardukite Catalogue = *Tablet S*

(strangely) belong to the earthly [*physical*] world.

2. White flowers bloom where blue flowers bloomed once before. The plants are wrong. Disorder hides beneath the leaves to secretly multiply and the signs become evident.

3. The Ten Kingdoms will come and go—*Babylon* and *Assyria:* the first and greatest. The *Aryan* follows thereafter, and then of *Egypt* and *Persia*, and so on the lakefront, then in the furthest eastward reach and then also the furthest western reach, and so on to the last Empire. Later, three new dawns (*ages*) will follow, but pass quickly, and are not of the Light.

4. The vibration that leads to Babylon...

5. The Darkness extinguished the Light again; and in turn, smothered itself.

6. Nearly all of the heroes have fallen in the end. Flowers no longer bloom—just strangling vines for refueling. The desert becomes an empty barren wasteland. In the branches of trees squat carrion birds who have already eaten the owls, who have already eaten the pigeons, that already ate the eagle.

7. Strange gray animals spawn from the ground. They gnaw at the roots of the trees until they fall over and with it the carrion birds. The gray animals then kill and eat the birds.

8. In deep recesses of the earth a blood-red animal

with red eyes germinates. It grows quickly. The strange gray creatures carry him food until it matures. Eventually it eats the creatures too.

9. At once there are no more empires of the world —until the afterbirth; and these are sick from their conception; led by the blood-red beast of the fields [*hills*]. Warfare dissolves them.

10-12. ...

13. By the twilight shadow of the true kingdom the red animal passes and the vines die with the world because it can hold nothing more.

14. Everywhere is heard a great crying, complaining and whining. The people drown in chaos and disorder—without an empire.

15. Now they cherish the Son of the Pure [*white*] flower and all happily submit to his reign in the new empire.

16. Many evil [*demons*] spirits have been born, but at the edge of the Light, the evil [*demon*] spirits melt away—the Light remains.

THE SAJAHA SERIES – TABLET IX[*]

1. Sajaha *(to Nebuchadnezzar II)*—Three are three visions that I want to share with you—each of them specific to a (*specific*) time.

---
[*] Mardukite Catalogue = *Tablet S*

2. The first image shows you a new king. He lives on shores of the lake. His family is related by blood to us. He sends many ships. He shapes the land such as has not been seen since the great *Sargon I*. He is learned and his gods are the same as ours.

3. The higher the new king rises in the world, the greater the envy and hatred is forged against him —gathering as a force it descends upon him as a terrible fight.

4. Eventually, the new king succumbs to the will of the majority. There is no trace of him—only secret knowledge remains.

5. Another King now reigns as the first of the world. It is not our blood and possesses no bright knowledge...

6. The second vision that I will share with you shows many people praying. Their minds blinded; they do not pray to the true God. They have concealed the once radiant Light in their temples – and inscribe falsehoods on the sacred tablets of their faith. They bring the wrong sacrifice to the temple. Signs from the gods become absent. Prayer and sacrifice turns to greed and bloody warfare.

7. Spirits turn sick and souls turn deformed and their new gods feast on their flesh and drink their blood.

8. Finally, the third vision shows how once again

a new king rises in the distance [*future*]. And this one is of our blood. His name is "*Hope*." After a period of peace, he perishes in war, and with him falls his name: "Hope."

9. The power of the Darkness overwhelms and takes over the world. The people make unclean temple sacrifices in their delusion. But the heirs of the heirs of Babylon, Assyria and Persia emerge, but the victory is far away; the new king is no more.

10 Many of the heirs rise up; suddenly—like a comet—their characters are realized, but the victory is far away; the new king is not there.

11. I am also in the way of seeing a strange vision: something like a enormous glowing wheel— and its spokes are people with no gender that are attached together. They breathe selfishness and become sickly slaves to the wheel...

12. I watch the enormous glowing wheel rolling over the ground bringing fire and inflaming the lands and sea. An evil noise—horrible and senseless—alarms everywhere at once, driving people into madness, increasing the intensity of chaos and confusion.

13. The people no longer recognize each other. Remote is a new king.

14-15. Yet another vision comes unbidden... I beheld the image of a beautiful golden goddess; and at first, I thought it was a portrait of Ishtar, although it was not in her usual likeness.

16. I took notice of a new king at the base of the Ishtar shrine—and a lot of people cheered him. As this Babylonian king makes a speech to his people, I almost thought a *New Babylon* was visible on the horizon—but I do not know if I behold an image of time past or the future.

17. I saw a bright sun shine on the city with the golden goddess; radiance spread throughout the whole country, upon the sea and the mountains—and everywhere there was great happiness and resounding celebration. As the sunlight blessed the *New Babylon*, the light of peace, love and unity spread far and wide among the people.

THE SAJAHA SERIES – TABLET X[*]

1. Sajaha—I see before me a starfire light at the ends of the sky—the lid of the water jug opening up to a new dawn (*marking the beginning of the Aquarian Age*).

2. A horror will befall all of the servants of Darkness and all their messengers. All their gold will melt to tears under the blinding radiance of *New Babylon*.

3. …

---

[*] Mardukite Catalogue = *Tablet S*

4. The righteous shall judge the unrighteous as the hour of the [*panthers*] will be against the [*dragon*] —the (giant) of the north against the desert worm.

5. Hypocrites rise—the defendant is the plaintiff; disorder turns to *Darkness*.

6. The Darkness embeds deeply beneath the people's skin—like a burrowing worm. The Light of the righteous becomes distorted; a fractured crystal speculum.

7. New Babylon will shine from the base of the mountain. And he who was the loneliest, will be the new king of Babylon, the king of the new kingdom empire of a new age.

THE SAJAHA SERIES – TABLET XI[*]

1. Sajaha—It is at that time a large flood over the high and once bright garden of the earth; and there will be no flood-waters, but a breath of decay everywhere.

2. From low gardens swarms of greedy beetles come up to eat their larvae under the flowering trees; The flowers of the trees wither—including their leaves. And still gluttonous beetles come. They do not have thoughts. No fire is thrown in order to burn new larvae. Thus the trees, bushes and grass fade away.

---

[*] Mardukite Catalogue = *Tablet S*

3. Everything dried up and everywhere things became bald. At mealtimes many of the greedy beetles die. The inhabitants of the bright gardens also starve.

4. The beetles outnumber the people and begin to feed on them.

5. Humans—their thinking and understanding is lost by a flood of foul omens. They could have protected their children, but since they lost the ability of understanding, they did not do anything.

6. The flood of decay in the bright gardens came before the flood of gluttonous beetles. And in such a way humans finally brought themselves their own bad end, because they bore this fate.

7. The first flood will come and pave the way for the second, at whose end extinction stands.

8. Then the beetles remaining in the lower gardens cease to thrive; without the seeds of the trees from above nothing prospers. This world dies and people from different countries no longer know each other. Enmity arises as the world is dying everywhere. In despair, the very last ones slay themselves.

9. This is the vision that I was given for the coming future. It is warning—not an inevitable fate. Cut the people off at the first flood. If your shot is a miss—know that you are all lost!

10. In order that you might recognize it, I want to

share images with you of the first coming flood, of which I spoke, more specifically. These pictures are colorful, strange and alien. They are left for the wise to interpret with understanding.

11. A white bird circled over the sea in the proximity of the noble and pure [*world*] mountain; it does no harm and produces no anger.

12. There are however numerous other birds – less noble and without the radiating whiteness – which envied the white one and flocked together against him, so it could not land and died of exhaustion and hunger, falling down from the clouds in the sky into a grave of the sea—and soon no one ever knew that it had existed.

13. The white bird drew its circles for a long time until its state of emergency forced it into battle against all of the others.

14. More comrades gathered and seized the white one after they had previously forced him to starve.

15. And there was again a lot of terrible struggles of the majority against the one. Finally, the white bird lay bleeding on the floor and could not fight back.

16. Because he had not yet sunk into the sea and was therefore still be seen by some of its white plumage, the others plucked him clean of feathers and devoured its raw meat.

17. Now the white bird was no longer. Soon they

learned he had been the leader of the *Starfire Light* —father of the white clouds of heaven. And from then on it was no longer pure light, and still just gray clouds, which stayed the rays of the sun and devoured their heat between heaven and earth.

18. But the numerous unladen birds that had survived the long struggle, now crying out loud, because it was cold and getting darker on the earth, and they said the white bird had been killed for the debt (of this) and so they perverted what was truth, and denied the guilt of their actions.

19. Time continued to pass; there came with the Dark evil [*demons*] spirits who feel at home in the dark. But with this came the illness of the spirit and the end of understanding.

20. For these dark demons are essentially unreal; they know no sorrow and no joy; they have no fear nor any other feelings. They lack all understanding and caring.

21. Some have realized that the white bird had also been protective shield against the dark power.

22. So, the envious birds slaughtered the Light that had come to protect against the Darkness.

23. And now they were all victims of the Lord of Shadows.

THE SAJAHA SERIES – TABLET XII[*]
Nebuchadnezzar Discourse – Part I

1. *Conversation between Sajaha and King Nebuchadnezzar II.*

2. Nebuchadnezzar—Speak to me, Sajaha, about the systems of this world. To what course does time take?

3. Sajaha—Darkness shall cover the sky over the whole world of space and time. For the worshipers of the evil spirit who are not completely destroyed, arise. They drill poisonous thorns into the bodies of the countries – the demon of evil they bring to your country, in your city of Light. Sunset is approaching us, because the darkness is strong in the world.

4. Nebuchadnezzar—Haven't I beaten the servants of darkness terribly? Destroyed their places? Burned the hell shrine? Executed priests and leaders? Imprisoned their superiors?

5. Sajaha—Oh, king, what good is it to root out the poisonous plant from the flowerbeds if its seeds are not destroyed?

6-7. Soon the day will come when you no longer recognize the bed of your garden. The flowers will be stifled—stalks of poisonous plants but will dominate.

---
[*] Mardukite Catalogue = *Tablet S*

8. The Light will go out through the dark shadows of the toxic stumps. This will feed from the pith of the precious flowers, which are now overgrown, no longer see the strength-giving rays of the sun. They are weakened and weakened again – until the evil of Darkness prevails almost completely.

9. Nebuchadnezzar – I intensely engaged with the emissaries of the dark spirit. But the king of Babylon is a righteous man, and he can show mercy to those who repent and renounce evil.

10. Sajaha—Oh, king, you hypocrites believed lies. Can thorns cease to sting? Can a poison stop being a poison? Can a lie not be a lie?

11. Oh, king, you love the good, and that's why you are looking for it. Your goodness hindered you in seeing the wickedness in full. Thus, goodness can be fooled and the emissaries of the Dark One bare much glamour—and you may have let many of them live.

12. Nebuchadnezzar—My faithful Sajaha, I am getting old and my attention turns to the next world. In my campaigns, I never praised myself, because after wisdom and brightness my spirit always longed for me and for my people.

13. The kingdom is powerful. I will give the one who is coming after me a strong Babylonia but the Third Sargon I was not.

14. Sajaha—The Third Sargon will come at a

later time. He will destroy the servants of Darkness and the seed of Darkness – he will uproot the evil by the roots.

15. He will have no mercy for any single one of the enemies of Light. He will spare none. He eradicates the sick souls and of the worshipers of Darkness, no trace will remain on the earth.

16. Terribly the third Sargon will be against everything that is hindering the development of the Clear Light.

17. He will purify the world; even out of ten people are killed—he wipes out everything that is wrong and everything that bears the mark of falsehood [*illusion*].

18-19. He will be ruthless to the Darkness. He will take the slain bodies and build high pyramids, then burn them.

20. The eternal order [*divine right*], which had been been lost, is restored—sent by transmissions from heaven (godhood) [*deity*].

21. Nebuchadnezzar—Oh, Sajaha, when will all this be?

22. Sajaha—From this day forward—as many years as have passed since the first Sargon.

23. The state of the earthly [*physical*] world will be bad.

24. But in the period of the third part of a year, the

Messenger will have done his work.

25. From the northern state he will come—appearing suddenly upon the earth; living in the venomous world; systems that he will shake with one blow and his power will be great.

26. He will not ask. He is not a seeker like those who follow him. He will simply *know*.

27. Then the Third Sargon will be the Light—The Messenger and the Third Sargon will Light up the world.

28. The righteous will wade in the blood of slaughtered unjust.

29. Until the work is done, the fires of destruction will burn from one end of the earth to the other.

30. All alone the true riches will remain.

31. Nebuchadnezzar—But does *New Babylon* come to exist?

31b. Sajaha—It will go down for a long time. It was only the Third Sargon that will again build it in the north country. There and then there will be a *New Babylon*.

32. Nebuchadnezzar—Will the *New Babylon* survive the times?

33. Sajaha—Oh, king, it will exist and reign in the Light for one-thousand years!

THE SAJAHA SERIES – TABLET XII[*]
Nebuchadnezzar Discourse – Part II

1. Nebuchadnezzar—Tell me what you see—What will happen to the people? What will be of the kingdom?

2. Sajaha—Things will worsen. But nothing can avert it—it already takes its course.

3-4. The way of the poison arrow circles the world. The sun darkens its Light from Chaldea to the base of the midnight mountain. But humans do not notice it – they are dazzled by a Light of falsehood; blinded by the reflection of fraudulently obtained gold.

5. Many property-owners [*noblemen*] fall; with cunning many frauds rise in their stead. Maliciously, a horrible breath operates most of your thoughts.

6. What is clear, collapses; what is unclean, thrives. What was below will be above; good and evil trade places.

7. The people will be drunk on confusion and madness reigns over the world.

8. Parents lose their children; children disown their parents. No longer are the voices of the gods heard—except for the lone righteous who will count for nothing in that time.

---
[*] Mardukite Catalogue = *Tablet S*

9. The nations will no longer know their meaning. Armies will fight against their commanders. Kings fall and temples turn to dust. Trash of ages resurfaces and debris reigns supreme.

10. All worldly [*physical*] power will be in the clutches of the unworthy. This will reverse the world.

11. Customs are no longer observed; vice is considered elegant. Men will operate with impunity toward boys—women will no longer want to be wives, but as men give themselves impunity, humans will mix themselves with animals and with impunity we witness hybrids. And the hybrids of hybrids will be in the streets of countless cities, without any exterminating them.

12-13. And the lowest will be elevated to the Supreme by the servants of the Dark One. The king interrupted the seer, shuddering.

14. Nebuchadnezzar—O Sajaha! Faithful counselor of your old king! Take pity on me and share a more pleasant picture for me to take to the *Otherworld*.

15. Sajaha—First must come the bad—and then the even more terrible.

16. For the Dark Lord will come upon the earth in human form—he will be worshiped by all of the emissaries of evil.

17-18. Previously, however, the evil must be

significantly fun in the earth [*physical*] world.

19. All that is bad, is regarded as good; everything that is good, is regarded as bad.

20. Humans will recognize no God. Gluttony and fornication, betrayal and deceit—these become their gods. They drink blood and wallow in slime.

21. Terrible lies they call truth, and the truth is not in them—except in the desert waiting longingly for the Third Sargon.

22. The first spark comes from the trampled ground of Chaldea. He will rise and fly, supported by fleeting clouds—the land of the north closest to the sky. The Third Sargon: From the battered Earth the liberator of Avengers rises!

23. Lands of the lonely righteous will stand up and form a huge storm that immediately strikes fire—moving forward it burns everywhere; everything evil everywhere.

24. Then the king raised both hands to the sky.

25. Nebuchadnezzar—Mighty they should be, the righteous and merciless!

26. Sajaha—So it will be!

THE SAJAHA SERIES – TABLET XII*
Nebuchadnezzar Discourse – Part III

1. The king went to Sajaha when he was old and tired and full of worries about his people and reign. Although Babylon was powerful and highly respected all over the world, the king felt that impending disaster threatening the future. Even his seer, Sajaha, had already predicted such. He went to inquire further.

2. Nebuchadnezzar—My dear faithful, Sajaha, tell me how it will be when the hour of light on the earth world returns if the times of the evil will be over and happy (hours) are spread out over my kingdom and the globe.

3. Sajaha—Since the victory of the righteous shall be first, the brave who persevered through all the shades of evil.

4. If the third Sargon will come and will have succeeded in battle, they will have victory against the prime majority.

5. He is the Avenger, his thundering over the earth with fiery chariots flashes until they are completely destroyed—dashing against the powers of *Darkness*.

6. After all of this, the earthly [*physical*] world will be cleansed of all evil and of all misery.

---

* Mardukite Catalogue = *Tablet S*

7. Numerous small groups of people will then inhabit the earthly [*physical*] world, but it will be the best world—a new golden age, which is lives and reign as *New Babylon*.

8. A tower will be built seven times higher than our E.TEMEN.AN.KI.

9. How beautiful and wonderful the world will be —the earth will shine. Dispute will not happen again. Greed is no longer know. Perversion and immorality is forgotten. Weapons are unnecessary.

10. And you, my king, will look over the top of the mountains to see the meeting of the world beyond. Then you will embrace joy.

11. Nebuchadnezzar—Remotely distant is the time. Lonely are the brave and the righteous. But ever is MARDUK with them!

THE SAJAHA SERIES – TABLET FRAGMENT* (EPILOGOS)

1. Sajaha—Let it be known my visions were blessed by the divine god, MARDUK. At the top of the god-mountain MARDUK reigns of this time. He sees bad omens; he cannot prevent this— it has been a long time coming. The shaft of his spear is stuck in the glass ceiling of the mountain.

2. The midnight country is caught in distress. The

---

* Mardukite Catalogue = *Tablet S*

bodies of fallen heroes rot at the foot of the holy mountain.

3. An Army of Darkness approach from the west, wild wallows approach from the east—the amount of the voiceless. Babylon is beyond saving; Assyria is no longer there to help.

4. Alone and mourning, MARDUK fixes his eyes upon the world from the mountain peaks. Lost is the home and gateway of the gods—Babylon. They no longer sing; they do not celebrate—yet they prepare for a fierce battle. And ISHTAR also cries for her people.

5. He listens to the voice [*sound*] of ISHTAR, Lord MARDUK, Protector of the Midnight Mountain! Push your spear at the enemy! Deliver our people from evil!

6. MARDUK replied to her: ISHTAR! How gladly would I do what you ask of me! But the people are to witness a crushed kingdom—numberless is the power of our enemies; the [*new*] Sargon, the Liberator, the Avenger, is not among them yet.

7. ISHTAR looked at him and said: MARDUK, see what has come up from below; that which once dominates our earthly [*physical*] world and the people, once came from above. We cannot tolerate upside-down domination of the world any longer! MARDUK, plunge your spear! The one who can wield the spear will be the new Sargon!

8. As Marduk pulled the spear out of the ground and threw it down as a force upon the world. And while MARDUK did this, ISHTAR told the stars to emit a new light: invisible.

9. On Earth, the spear of MARDUK had its effect on the world: A new purpose he delivered to the people; a new weapon and passion—a new Sargon took stewardship of the people, and soon took the spear of MARDUK.

10. A mighty struggle began—until the bottom was defeated and increased and was built at the top of *New Babylon*.

Look for all this at a future time; all of this will be.

AVAILABLE FROM THE **JOSHUA FREE** PUBLISHING IMPRINT

THE COMPLETE BOOK OF MARDUK BY NABU

A Pocket Anunnaki Devotional Companion to Babylonian Rituals

edited by Joshua Free

10th Anniversary
Collector's Edition
Hardcover
Mardukite Liber-W

THE MAQLU RITUAL BOOK

A Pocket Companion to Babylonian Exorcisms, Banishing Rites & Protective Spells

edited by Joshua Free

10th Anniversary
Collector's Edition
Hardcover
Mardukite Liber-M

WOULD YOU LIKE TO KNOW MORE ???

Take the first steps on the
Pathway to Self-Honesty
with your next book by Joshua Free...

TABLETS OF DESTINY
USING ANCIENT WISDOM TO UNLOCK HUMAN POTENTIAL

AVAILABLE FROM THE **JOSHUA FREE** PUBLISHING IMPRINT

SYSTEMOLOGY
The Pathway to Self-Honesty

GO FURTHER AND BE

CRYSTAL CLEAR

CRYSTAL CLEAR

The Self-Actualization Manual & Guide to Total Awareness

by Joshua Free
Foreword by Kyra Kaos

Take control of your destiny
and chart the first steps
toward your own spiritual evolution.
Realize new potentials of the
Human Condition with
a Self-guiding handbook for
Self-Processing toward
Self-Actualization
in Self-Honesty using actual
techniques and training
provided for the coveted
"Mardukite Systemology Grade-III
Self-Defragmentation Course Program"
—once only available
directly and privately from
the underground Systemology Society.

Discover the amazing power behind the
applied spiritual technology
used for counseling and advisement in
the tradition of Mardukite Zuism.

1995 **JOSHUA FREE** **2020**

PUBLISHED BY THE **JOSHUA FREE** IMPRINT REPRESENTING

The Founding Church of Mardukite Zuism

mardukite.com

www.ingramcontent.com/pod-product-compliance
Lightning Source LLC
Chambersburg PA
CBHW011141290426
44108CB00023B/2709